THE GREATEST PODCAST MARKETING BOOK *EVER WRITTEN*

A Proven Marketing and Sales Strategy For Busy Business Owners Who Are Looking To Attract More Leads and Sales To Their Business WITHOUT BREAKING THE BANK!

Disclaimer

As a book on podcast marketing, while every effort has been made to ensure the content is accurate and up to date, the author makes no warranties or representations regarding the currency, accuracy, or completeness of the information provided.

The author will not be liable for any financial loss or commercial damages, including but not limited to consequential, incidental, special, or other damages resulting from your actions or inactions.

Examples, estimates, and results reflect the author's personal experiences and those of selected clients. They should not be interpreted as a promise or guarantee that you will earn money, gain new leads, or generate sales after completing this book or implementing any of the strategies, systems, and processes described.

Your results depend on the time you invest in learning and applying the ideas, tools, and techniques presented, as well as your financial investment, knowledge level, and other relevant skills necessary to achieve your podcast marketing goals.

You are responsible for any actions taken as a result of reading this book. Before implementing any ideas found here, please conduct your due diligence and seek professional legal advice as needed.

In this heartfelt dedication, I celebrate my dear friend Kerin. This book is a testament to the profound impact you have had on my life. Your technical brilliance and keen insight have illuminated my path, given me courage, and shown me the importance of discipline, action, and perseverance. Thank you for your unwavering friendship and for being a remarkable source of inspiration.

Foreword

On my 25th birthday I was given responsibility over a portfolio of blue-chip stocks that had been created for me years earlier. This portfolio was to get me through college, graduate school and give me a good start financially. As you can imagine, there was absolutely no way that I was going to risk losing any of this six figure windfall. Some nine years later, this same portfolio was generating nearly five times my full-time employment salary.

It was at this time that I started a private investment management company with two clients and less than a million dollars under active management. The thrust of my management was different, emphasizing income production while taking advantage of both short-term market volatility and longer-term cyclical movements. Disciplined quality, diversification, income production, and profit taking guidelines brought income independence to clients that stuck with the program.

On May 1st, 2023, I accepted "an offer you can't refuse" for my $110 million company, knowing that I was going to dedicate my time to sharing this unique, high quality, process with as many investors as I could. There were four phases to this adventure: The Retirement Income Coach LLC was created, "Retirement Money Secrets: A Financial Insider's Guide to Income Independence" was published, theincomecoach.net website was developed, and spreading the word about all three began on social media and by appearing on a selection of top tier podcasts.

Podcasts, particularly “The My Future Business Show” allowed me to spread the word, face-to-face, to tens of thousands of people. New investors, retirees, professionals, even investment professionals are getting the message about a better way to achieve their income independence goals. This “show” was particularly innovative in its focus on my message. From preparation through to implementation of a mission focused interview session, my message, and mine alone was what listeners received. Not only was it powerful and cost-effective, it worked at getting me in front of my target audience. This is what effective podcast marketing looks like.

Rick, without being “salesy” or overly promotional, helped me sell my book, my coaching services, and investing concepts, while expressing an authentic interest in the approach to the safer and more income productive investing style that we were talking about. The interview flew by in what seemed like minutes, and there is no doubt that my message is valuable to all who watch the “Retirement Money Secrets” episode.

Effective soft-sell advertising is what you want from a podcast interview. And given what I know about Rick's approach to getting results for his guests, I know for sure that “The Greatest Podcast Marketing Book Ever Written" will give both new and experienced guests a cost-effective promotional edge that brings out their very best.

If you’re a business owner who’s looking for a cost-effective way to promote your business, then "The Greatest Podcast Marketing Book Ever Written” is for you. This book not only makes podcast interviews interesting, enjoyable, and productive, it demonstrates that podcast marketing delivers results.

Steve Selengut - Author and Income Coach

"The Journey of a Thousand Miles

***Begins With One Step"* - Lao Tzu**

Table of Content

Preface

I believe the failure rate among small to medium-sized businesses is unacceptably high. As an experienced marketer, business builder, and podcaster, I am committed to addressing this issue.

With more individuals moving away from traditional employment toward entrepreneurship, I aim to help you incorporate conversion-focused podcast guest interviews into your marketing strategy, ensuring long-term prosperity.

I wrote this book to assist motivated business owners like you in filling their sales pipeline with double the number of targeted prospects each month. This will enable you to make more sales, enjoy your after-hours, enhance your quality of life, and grow your bottom line without relying on outdated marketing tactics that don't work.

To fully benefit from this system, you need three key elements:

Commitment

A Clear Road Map

Someone to Guide You

If you're seeking results, you've come to the right place. This book provides step-by-step instructions to help you set up your interview marketing system, differentiate your business, establish your authority in your niche, and consistently attract new leads and paying customers.

Introduction

Hi, my name is Rick Nuske, and I'm thrilled you found this book on podcast marketing. As the host of the popular business-building podcast, The My Future Business Show, I've had the privilege of building strong relationships with hundreds of outstanding professionals. Many of these talented individuals have sought advice on maximizing results from their guest interview content.

If you're a busy business owner looking for an effective way to attract new prospects, promote your business, increase sales, and lower customer acquisition costs, you're in the right place. This book outlines the exact steps you need to follow to achieve these results through podcast guest interviews.

I've researched how individuals conduct themselves and analyzed each aspect of the guest interview process. From this analysis, I've identified specific steps you can take to achieve better business results.

I've compiled this information into a 3-step framework for you to use. Within this framework, you will find step-by-step instructions that will help you select the right podcasts to appear on and guide you in preparing for and delivering persuasive interviews that generate consistent leads and sales.

A Little Secret

Here's a little secret about this book: it was never meant to be the greatest podcast marketing book ever written. The aim behind the title was to spark curiosity and encourage thought among potential readers. It was crafted to grab attention and prompt readers to explore the content to uncover the insights and strategies within. Ultimately, this catchy title serves as a starting point for a deeper conversation about podcast marketing as an essential promotional tool for your business.

To illustrate the importance of gaining attention for your business, marketing expert Gary Vaynerchuk emphasizes in his book "Day Trading Attention" that attention is the most valuable currency for marketers in today's information-overloaded world. He explains that capturing and retaining your target audience's attention helps your brand stand out and create meaningful connections with potential customers. This concept aligns perfectly with podcast marketing, where your content can captivate listeners, encourage genuine engagement, and build real trust with your target audience.

About halfway through developing the original outline for this book, I started listening to another audiobook titled "Perennial Seller" by Ryan Holiday. In this book, Ryan explores the art and strategy of creating timeless, evergreen works that endure in a fast-changing market. He emphasizes the importance of crafting content that transcends trends and remains relevant long after its creation. In the context of podcast marketing, the principles from "Perennial Seller" highlight the need to write a book that delivers lasting value, addresses timeless topics, and resonates with audiences well beyond its release date.

The goal of this book has always been to make a lasting impact. It aims to help you capture and hold attention, build a loyal following, and demonstrate how to create a strong brand presence that endures beyond temporary marketing trends. This book is designed to be a source of lasting relevance that offers long-term benefits for your business.

With this goal in mind, each morning I thought about how to write this book, The Greatest Podcast Marketing Book Ever Written, to ensure it became an essential resource for busy business owners. Now that the book is complete, I can confidently say that no stone was left unturned.

I'm excited to share what I know about attracting attention and making sales through podcast marketing. I hope you can use this information to develop your unique podcast marketing system, secure interviews on the right shows, deliver outstanding performances, and build a library of valuable interview content. This content will help educate your target audience for years to come and, importantly, inspire listeners to become buyers of your products and services.

"*When the Why starts to grow,*

the How gets simpler" **- Jim Rohn**

Roadmap

To achieve success with podcast guest interviews, it's essential to understand how they work and implement each step outlined in this book. This will help you create a specific action plan leading up to, during, and after each interview.

In the opening section, I introduce podcasting and podcast guest interviews while explaining your role as a guest. I also discuss why podcast interviews are a powerful way to build awareness and excitement about the solution your business offers. I make a strong case for adopting podcast interviews as your primary marketing strategy, highlighting how guest appearances can address many of your marketing challenges.

To guide you through the entire guest interview process, I've created a 'roadmap' for you to follow. This roadmap includes everything you need to research and select the right podcasts that align with your marketing goals. It also outlines the process for booking yourself as a guest and highlights critical elements necessary for delivering persuasive interviews that meet both your target audience's needs and your business's marketing objectives.

In writing this book, I believe my greatest achievement is simplifying conversion-focused podcast interview marketing. As you work through the book, please focus on one section at a time, and only move on when you feel confident in your understanding.

If you're ready to harness the power of podcast interviews to promote your business, book, or venture and attract a steady stream of leads and potential customers, let's begin with a quick look at the 3-step Podcast Marketing Roadmap.

Instructions

The Podcast Marketing System is made up of three main parts, and covers...

Before The Interview

During The Interview

After The Interview

Inside each of the 3 main parts there are 3 sub-parts. Each sub-part contains action items.

At the end of the book, there's a link to your PODCAST MARKETING SPREADSHEET. This spreadsheet contains all of the steps and action items described throughout this book.

To access the spreadsheet, save a copy. As you work your way through each part of the book, open your spreadsheet, go to the relevant section, and update it when that section is complete.

Further resources are provided as links inside the provided spreadsheet.

Don't skip any part of this book, they are all important. Read each part, implement what you learn, and contact me if you have any questions.

Before The Interview

Attention Marketing

In his influential book "Day Trading Attention," Gary Vaynerchuk emphasizes the crucial role of capturing attention in today's crowded online landscape. He points out the vast amount of content that individuals and businesses compete against every day, making it more challenging to stand out and connect with your target audience.

Yet, even in the midst of intense competition, my extensive experience testing various marketing strategies has taught me one undeniable truth: as long as there is a demand for your solution, podcast marketing will remain a valuable part of your promotional strategy. The unique format of podcasting allows for deep engagement, fostering a genuine connection between you, the creators, and their audience, which is often difficult to achieve through other media.

This belief drives my commitment to helping you build and utilize the benefits of a comprehensive podcast marketing system, which aims to capture attention and sustain interest, turning it into valuable leads and a consistent stream of conversions.

To make a clear and effective point, conversion becomes much easier when your target audience wants what you offer. While providing high-quality products and services is crucial, your podcast marketing strategy will fail without an engaged and interested audience. Without an audience seeking what you offer, there are no leads; without leads, there are no sales; and without sales, there is no business.

Thankfully, attracting attention is now easier than ever, enabling you to reach your target audience through various methods. For instance, some marketers achieve success with paid advertising. However, a downside to paid marketing is that when providers increase their prices to meet demand, advertising costs also rise.

While I know people who have succeeded with paid ads, I don't believe they are the only path to achieve results. For me, paid ads are expensive, complicated, and often ineffective. In contrast, podcast marketing is a reliable and effective way to gain attention, build interest, and motivate people to take action—without relying on paid advertising.

To those who dismiss organic traffic tactics, I want to highlight some advantages of podcast marketing over paid advertising. First and foremost, aside from the time you invest, creating podcast content is much cheaper than paid advertising. This saving is especially crucial for small businesses with limited marketing budgets.

Not only can podcast marketing be profitable and cost-effective, it also has the potential to remain timeless. In contrast, the attention gained from paid advertising disappears as soon as you stop spending money. By investing time to create interview content, you develop marketing assets that continue delivering value over a longer period of time without the financial commitment.

Podcast marketing also boosts your brand's credibility and trustworthiness, making it an important factor in its effectiveness. Without trust and credibility, attracting buyers becomes even more of a challenge. When done right, podcast marketing builds an audience that is familiar with your content and trusts you enough to take the next step toward becoming a lead, customer or client.

Additionally, people who are looking for solutions your business offers can easily access your content to learn more. As a result, your content is likely to be shared among individuals and circulated multiple times, creating a much sought after viral effect.

Trust-Based Selling

Can you remember the last time a stranger called you to sell something? How did you feel during that call? Did you feel so positive about the experience that you wanted to pull out your credit card and buy whatever they were offering? I'd guess probably not.

Now, imagine if your last conversation with someone didn't revolve around a sales pitch. Instead, it focused on helping you solve your biggest problem. How would you react to that? This scenario is not only more memorable for all the right reasons, but it would also be much more effective at motivating you to take a step closer to making a purchase, which is the ultimate goal of podcast marketing.

Trust-based selling is crucial to your interview strategy and requires you to set aside outdated sales techniques. The "sell at all costs" approach simply doesn't work in an interview setting.

As the host of The My Future Business Show, I have had the privilege of learning from the world's leading authority in trust-based selling, Ari Galper. Ari has clients in 35 countries and has worked with notable figures such as Richard Branson and Joan Rivers. He has also been featured in various books, including Dan Kennedy's No BS series and Perry Marshall's 80/20 Sales and Marketing.

I chose to talk about Ari because his ability to build trust is unmatched, and I know you'll benefit from his methods. For instance, shortly after scheduling an interview with Ari as my guest, I received an unexpected package on my doorstep. This package was from Ari, who refers to it as a 'trust box.' Inside, I found his books Unlock the Sales Game, Trusted Authority, The One Sales Call, Lessons from Toby, and an innovative flipbook-style video player the size of an A5 book that I had never seen before.

Although Ari's gift positively impacted me, it also made me feel as if I had known him for much longer than I actually had. By sharing deep insights and personal stories through his video player and books, I couldn't help but feel a sense of familiarity with Ari, which I believe is key to building trust.

Fast forward a week, and here I was online with Ari, discussing his book, "Unlock the Sales Game". For the most part, Ari is just like you and me. However, what stood out was his emphasis on trust, integrity, and authenticity in everything he does. The great thing about Ari's approach is that it works no matter where you are in the world, and importantly, it's easy to apply.

As Ari states, "our customers need to know who they're talking to, they need to know we know what we're talking about, and they need to know we can be trusted to do the job they need us to do." He adds that "in this new economy, trust is a currency everyone understands." Therefore, I encourage you to focus on building trust during your interviews and to delve deeply into every conversation to bring out your best and deliver the most value.

From your very first interview and from that day forward, you must concentrate on establishing real trust while letting go of the need to make a sale. Remember, your interviews should serve as a vehicle for delivering value, not for making sales. The natural selling process follows once you've built deep trust with your audience. They will then recognize their needs and reach out for your help to solve their problems.

As Ari points out, "the thing about trust-based selling is that when you stop actively selling and focus on building trust and helping your audience clarify their problems, you become unique, and people start to notice that you're different." This is how I felt when I received Ari's trust box in the mail. I felt an instant connection and, importantly, that I could trust Ari to do the right thing.

Just as Ari sends a trust box to establish an initial connection, you can share similar trust box-type content in physical form, as a digital download, on an FAQ page, or as a video. This information effectively introduces you, breaks down barriers, and provides just enough insight about you and what you do without explicitly detailing how you can solve their problems.

Podcast Marketing

As far back as I can remember, books have played a significant role in my life. From the early days when my Nana read me bedtime stories to the moment I discovered my first Harry Potter book, I have always been captivated by books and their stories.

I've continued reading books because they are a great source of ideas and inspiration. I gauge a book's value by whether it includes at least one useful takeaway. Nearly every business or self development book I've read or listened to has provided insights and ideas that have improved my personal and professional success.

As I started writing this book, I recognized that the insights and ideas within these pages could be something special that helps you succeed. If you can take away even one useful idea and achieve a result from it, I will have accomplished my ultimate goal of helping you transform your business through podcast marketing.

Given the many amazing books I've read over the years, I wondered if there was one takeaway I could share to inspire you and serve as a strong introduction to this book. After a lengthy search, I rediscovered "The Go-Giver" by Bob Burg, which perfectly captures the essence of this work.

In reading this book, I was reminded that podcasting—especially podcast marketing—is all about giving in order to receive, not giving with the expectation of getting something back. Reflecting on the old proverb "give and you shall receive," I recognized the importance of prioritizing others. With this guiding principle in mind, I wrote this book to serve you, help you build a lasting business, and share insights that can enrich your personal and professional life for years to come.

So, the first question I have for you is: what do you know about podcasting and podcast marketing? If you don't know much, that's okay. Soon, you'll gain a complete understanding and a new appreciation for why business owners need an effective way to connect with their target audience and maintain that connection.

I don't know if you've noticed, but in today's digital age, attention spans are shorter than ever, and traditional advertising methods are becoming increasingly expensive and less effective. This is why I believe many entrepreneurs, authors, and business owners are seeking new ways to connect with their ideal prospects and generate sales.

Just imagine having the best solution in the world but lacking a cost-effective way to attract, educate, and market it to your ideal customers. Without an affordable, efficient, and reliable method to generate a steady stream of qualified leads and buyers, your business could easily fall into a feast-or-famine cycle—or worse, risk going out of business entirely.

With these points in mind, many business owners are launching their own branded podcasts to attract their target audience. While branded podcasting enables businesses to engage with their audience on a more personal level, what should a busy business owner do if they lack the time or desire to start and maintain their own show?

If you're a busy business owner, sharing your knowledge and experience on other people's podcasts can be a great option. This strategy helps you build trust, establish your expertise, and create a genuine connection with listeners. By providing informative content on another show, you position yourself as a thought leader and foster a positive association with your brand. Plus, being a guest on others' shows requires much less time and effort.

Now, even if you're excited about what I've just shared, it's important to have a clear understanding of the entire interview process before scheduling your first one. While guest interviews aren't overly complicated, there are several factors you should know beforehand. This knowledge will help streamline the process and increase your chances of securing a spot on valuable shows.

The next question is: What do you hope to achieve by appearing on different podcasts? Are you looking to increase brand awareness, generate leads, or drive sales? By clearly defining your goals upfront, you can tailor your interview content to align with your priorities and target shows that focus on your preferred topics.

The beauty of knowing what you want and why you want it is that it provides clarity from the start. This clarity gives you the direction needed to create focused interview content that aligns with your business goals. When you understand the specifics of what you aim to achieve, you'll be ready to research, reach out to hosts, and book guest interviews.

Now, before we dive into the details of this book, let me address the elephant in the room. Your guest interviews are not sales presentations. For this system to work effectively, you must never pitch your products or services during any interviews.

Returning to Bob Burg and The Go-Giver, your interview should focus on giving value without expecting anything in return. This approach may seem counterintuitive, but trust me when I say that it is the key to achieving results.

When executed effectively, guest interviews can serve as a powerful promotional tool that distinguishes your business from the competition. You will educate those looking for solutions to specific problems while establishing your business as the top choice in the marketplace.

Why Podcast Marketing?

As an example of podcasting's utility, average commute times have increased in recent years, leading many commuters to turn to podcasts for entertainment and learning during their daily travels. Today's vehicles often come equipped with built-in podcast features, allowing drivers to enjoy their favorite podcasts without needing smartphones or additional digital media devices.

This portability has made podcasts an invaluable platform for individuals and businesses to share their ideas, opinions, and experiences with a much larger audience while keeping costs low. Unlike traditional advertising methods, which can be expensive and less personal, podcasts create a more intimate connection with listeners.

One of the primary reasons podcast interviews are so effective in generating leads and driving sales is their ability to engage a highly targeted audience that is genuinely interested in the content being presented. This level of engagement not only enhances brand visibility but also builds trust and credibility with potential customers.

By sharing insightful discussions and expert interviews, you can position yourself as a thought leader in your industry, ultimately leading to increased customer loyalty and higher conversion rates. In a content-driven world, podcasts stand out as a powerful medium to create meaningful connections and drive business growth.

Unlike other forms of marketing on platforms like Facebook, Google, and LinkedIn, podcast listeners are already interested in the content they consume. This means they are more likely to pay attention to your message, making it easier for you to connect with them at the end of the interview.

Podcast interviews are also a smart business decision because they keep your content relevant and accessible over time, making much of it evergreen. Evergreen content is not tied to specific dates or trends, allowing listeners to discover and benefit from these interviews months or even years after their initial release.

This long-term accessibility can generate consistent traffic to your business, enhancing your brand's visibility and authority in your niche. Additionally, evergreen interviews can be repurposed into various formats, such as blog posts, social media snippets, or video highlights, maximizing their reach and utility.

Your podcast interviews not only allow you to showcase your business but also your personality. They provide a chance to add a human element to your brand, where you can share stories, experiences, and insights in a personal and authentic way.

However, before you can propose solutions to someone's problems, they need to know enough about you to feel they can trust you. Building trust is essential for success in podcast interviews, and it's crucial to recognize how important trust is to your audience. You gain trust by showing up consistently, speaking your truth, keeping your promises, and offering practical solutions to their problems.

"*If you want to get known, spend zero dollars on advertising, and do it as fast as possible, you need to get on podcasts*" **- Grant Cardone**

Podcast Marketing Strategy

To illustrate the importance of effective marketing, let's consider the publishing world. Each year, thousands of new titles are released, but many quickly fade into obscurity. Several factors contribute to this, including poor distribution and average writing, but one major reason is often ineffective marketing.

Imagine investing countless hours and tremendous effort into a book, only to see it fail due to inadequate exposure and reach. Without a strong marketing system that effectively converts curiosity into commitment, even the best books can go unnoticed.

With this in mind, the primary goal of your podcast marketing strategy is to make your audience aware of a problem they might not realize they have and to inspire them to seek solutions and take action. When the right people listen to your engaging interviews and recognize their value, they are motivated to act and are more likely to share their new insights with others in their network.

Your interview strategy must outline how you will conduct guest interviews, and detail the steps you will take to encourage listeners to take action, including timing for those actions. This process begins with dedicating time to identify the problems faced by your target audience and developing an interview schedule that addresses most, if not all, of those issues throughout your interview campaign. Additionally, your interview strategy acts as a structured guide for each interview, ensuring that you never cover the same topic in more than one interview.

As you regularly participate in more podcast interviews, you'll gradually expand your influence and build a larger network. Each interview will serve as a platform to help more people by sharing knowledge and showcasing your expertise. Over time, this expanding circle of influence increases awareness of you, your business, and the valuable solutions you offer.

However, while participating in interviews is a vital way to enhance your visibility, it's important to understand that this effort alone won't necessarily turn listeners into customers or clients. For your strategy to be truly effective, each interview must be part of a well-structured podcast marketing funnel that guides potential customers through each step of your “buyer's journey”. Specific funnel details are provided in the systems section of this book.

For your business to thrive, generating sales is essential. Thus, setting up your podcast marketing funnel should be a priority, ideally before your first interview. This proactive approach lets you book interviews with confidence, knowing you have a system in place that nurtures engagement and builds relationships with potential customers who come to know, like, and trust you.

Although building your own podcast marketing funnel is not overly difficult, it is a key part of your podcast guest strategy that will serve its purpose at the conclusion of each interview. By combining your guest interviews with a well-structured marketing funnel, you can systematically improve your promotional efforts, increase customer engagement, and boost conversions.

The ultimate goal is to create a dynamic system that continuously promotes your business, book, or project even after your interview ends. Your interviews attract new customers and clients while generating ongoing interest in your offers. Meanwhile, your funnel automates the subsequent steps in the buyer's journey. The more relevant and effective your funnel is, the better it converts leads into sales in the background, allowing you to focus on other areas of your business.

Podcast interviews are a long-term growth strategy that should be a key component of your promotional efforts. A well-thought-out guest interview strategy is an effective way to build brand awareness and trust. It also helps establish you as an authority, attracting a consistent flow of leads and sales without relying on traditional sales techniques.

I want to emphasize the importance of adopting a systematic approach to podcast marketing. By carefully planning your strategy, not only will you gain clarity and focus, you'll be better prepared for each interview, and create content that connects with your target audience. Importantly, you'll have a system in place that automates much of the subsequent interaction with prospects.

By appearing on shows with a narrow focus, you can reach a targeted and engaged audience. For instance, if you sell fitness equipment, you can book yourself on a health and fitness podcast to discuss relevant topics. This way, you connect with an audience that is not only interested in health and fitness but also likely to be interested in the solutions you offer.

As listeners engage with your authentic and informative interviews, they will begin to develop a genuine connection with your brand, making them more receptive to learning about your products or services. This organic, non-sales approach enables a seamless transition from awareness to consideration of your solution, ultimately boosting conversions from listeners to leads and from leads to sales.

Podcast Marketing Goals

While your interview strategy guides the preparation and execution of each guest interview, your interview goals provide clear direction and purpose for your participation. This focus helps you achieve your desired outcomes for each guest appearance. By combining a well-defined interview strategy with specific goals, you can consistently create interview content that your target audience seeks, rather than having unpredictable results.

By establishing your goals beforehand, you gain a clear perspective on what you need to do to prepare for each interview. You will know the mindset needed during the call and can plan each interview to ensure it makes sense and delivers value from start to finish. This typically involves deciding how to navigate the interview, identifying your core message, creating a story arc, providing relevant examples, and showcasing your expertise in a way that impresses the audience and leaves them eager to learn more about your solutions.

It's essential to identify your goals before booking guest interviews. Document the specific outcomes you want to achieve in each interview, and clarify what you want listeners to do afterward. Your goal could be to share success stories from current customers, introduce a new solution to a problem your target audience faces, or establish your authority in a new market. You might also aim to raise brand awareness, grow your email subscriber list, position yourself as an industry expert, or network with others in your field to expand your reach.

When you have clear goals, your interview campaign becomes purpose-driven and engaging, leaving a positive lasting impression on your target audience. Understanding what your audience wants, what you want, and how you plan to achieve those outcomes increases the likelihood of moving listeners to the next stage in your promotional funnel.

When you've identified goals for each of your interviews, document them. Create a simple spreadsheet to list all the problems and common questions, detailing how and when you will tackle each one during your interview campaign. Use this list to inform hosts about the topics you want to discuss, enabling you to schedule interviews to cover each subject. You will find a spreadsheet for this purpose in the resources section of this book.

Always treat your interviews as a lead magnet and refrain from promoting your products and services during the call. Your focus should be solely on delivering value throughout the conversation. The last thing you want is for your interviews to feel like pitch fests, as this does not inspire listeners to take action.

However, there is an appropriate time, usually toward the end of the interview, when you can share your call-to-action, encouraging listeners to access more information about your solutions. The main focus needs to be on improving how you share information and stories that naturally guide listeners toward making their own decision about your offer.

What Problem Are You Solving?

Knowing your target audience's pain points gives you a competitive edge during interviews. Discussing their challenges and addressing them is crucial for offering relevant value, which in turn generates interest in your solutions. By focusing on their pain points, you will position yourself on podcasts that attract an audience seeking the solutions your business offers.

Addressing pain points involves more than just talking about your solutions. It requires sharing relevant stories that show your understanding of their problems. This approach allows you to present your solution without coming across as overly salesy. Clear and concise messaging is essential, as it highlights how your solution directly addresses their pain points and offers a better alternative than your competitors.

Your target audience's pain points drive their decisions and influence their purchasing behavior. By identifying and addressing these issues during your interviews, you can confidently discuss them and position your business as the solution for providing customers with what they are looking for.

When sharing your stories, consider the emotional impact on your audience as you address their pain points. While providing a practical solution is important, focusing on the emotional needs of your target audience can create a deeper connection and foster brand loyalty. For example, a business that sells cleaning products could address the time-consuming nature of cleaning by emphasizing how their products allow customers to enjoy more time with family or pursue hobbies.

Introduction To Interviews

If you're new to podcast interviews, here's a quick overview. Podcast guest interviews typically involve two participants: the host and you, the guest. These interviews can last anywhere from thirty minutes to an hour.

During the interview, you'll have several opportunities to share your knowledge, insights, and experiences with both the host and their audience. By providing valuable information and engaging in meaningful conversation, you can quickly establish yourself as an expert in your niche.

Considering the time required for a host to produce a single interview, it's clear why the podcast guest interview strategy is appealing. Recording, editing, and distributing a thirty-minute interview can take over five hours. Given your existing workload, managing your own podcast requires a significant time commitment. Therefore, it makes sense for many business owners to focus their promotional efforts on a guest interview strategy that yields quicker results.

The advantage of podcast interviews is that over time, you gain recognition for your expertise. When you're featured on a show, both you and your business receive an immediate boost in credibility and authority. As more hosts discover you, they will start inviting you to be a guest on their shows, allowing you to reach an even larger audience with your message.

Adding Value

The key to achieving results with your podcast interviews is adding a ton of value without expecting anything in return, which enhances every interaction with you and your business. And in the context of this book, this means providing as much value as possible before, during, and after each interview.

Entrepreneurs and business owners who dedicate time to educating their clients and providing value upfront often succeed in building strong relationships and credibility. By informing their potential customers, these successful individuals improve their brand image and cultivate a loyal customer base that appreciates their content, focus, and additional effort.

So, rather than concentrating on aspects like your website's design or the polish of your sales copy, focus on adding value at every stage of your prospect's journey. Deliver value before, during, and after each interaction to engage and excite your potential customers.

When you shift your focus from what you can gain to how you can add value before, during, and after each interview, you create a strong foundation to promote your business, book, or venture. This change in focus will inspire your audience to engage and become leads and customers.

By regularly overdelivering, your audience will feel encouraged to express their appreciation by becoming leads or making purchases. This creates a continuous value cycle that will benefit both your audience and your business.

In my earlier example, I shared how Ari Galper surprised me with a physical gift. This unexpected gesture left a positive impression. One of the best ways to deliver exceptional value is by surprising your audience. Can you recall the last time a business genuinely surprised you with something unexpected? Was it memorable? Keeping that in mind, aim to create a similarly positive experience for your future customers by adding as much value as possible. When someone shares how you provided value and helped them overcome an issue, it attracts others who face similar challenges.

"*People are more willing to say yes to us if we have first given them something that benefits them.*" - Robert Cialdini

Influence and Persuasion

When I first started learning about marketing and sales, I only knew that they worked together to attract new customers. Since I needed more customers at the time, I began to learn everything I could to bring them to my business. In marketing, I learned the basics of market research, advertising, and branding. In sales, I discovered how to turn listeners into leads and leads into customers.

Although I learned a lot about marketing and sales, I still didn't know much about human behavior. I didn't believe it was relevant to podcast marketing until I discovered Dale Carnegie's book, "How to Win Friends and Influence People." This book sparked my interest in understanding the psychology of influence and persuasion, and how to apply them ethically in my business.

Shortly after reading Carnegie's book, I came across Robert Cialdini's "Influence: The Psychology of Persuasion," which offers a strong foundation for an effective podcast marketing strategy. Although many authors have helped shape my success, Cialdini's book is one of the best on influence and persuasion.

On the following pages, I've summarized what I've learned about Cialdini's principles: reciprocity, commitment and consistency, social proof, authority, liking, scarcity, and unity. When used strategically, each of these principles can greatly improve your results. They can guide your actions before, during, and after each podcast appearance, leaving a lasting impression on your target audience.

Reciprocity

The principle of reciprocity is based on the idea that people feel obligated to return favors. When someone does something for us, we naturally want to reciprocate. For example, if you provide exceptional value before, during, and after each interview, the people you interact with will likely feel indebted and want to return the favor. They may show their appreciation by subscribing to your newsletter, providing feedback through a review or testimonial, or purchasing your product or service.

Reciprocity is essential in podcast interviews, as it involves exchanging value between you and the host for the benefit of their audience. When you share valuable insights, expertise, or engaging stories during the interview, it creates a sense of indebtedness in the host. This can lead to the host promoting your interview, recommending your products and services, and often inviting you to return to their show.

Reciprocity promotes collaboration, strengthens relationships, and enhances your podcast guest profile. By grasping the concept of reciprocity and engaging in mutually beneficial exchanges with the host and their audience, you can boost the quality of your podcast appearances, broaden your audience reach, and create valuable connections that open doors to new opportunities.

Case Study - Reciprocity

As an example, let's look at a business owner who is a guest on a popular entrepreneurship podcast. During the interview, the guest shares valuable insights on effective marketing strategies, tips for business growth, and personal stories about overcoming challenges in the industry. The host appreciates the guest's expertise, and the engaging conversation resonates with the audience, generating positive feedback.

After the podcast interview, the guest sends a personalized thank-you email to the host, expressing gratitude for the opportunity to be on the show. They also offer to provide additional resources or support for future episodes. The guest shares the podcast episode on their social media platforms, tagging the host and highlighting their collaboration. This gesture not only shows appreciation for the host's show but also expands the episode's reach to a broader audience.

As a result of this activity, the host is impressed by the guest's professionalism, proactive attitude, and willingness to support their show. In return, the host features the guest in their newsletter, invites them to participate in upcoming panel discussions, and recommends them for guest appearances on other industry-related shows. This mutually beneficial relationship enhances visibility, credibility, and networking opportunities for both the guest and the host within the podcasting community and beyond.

Commitment and Consistency

Now that we've addressed reciprocity, let's move on to Cialdini's principle of commitment and consistency. This principle is key in shaping interactions during podcast interviews, impacting both you and the host. It suggests that individuals have a strong urge to act in line with their past commitments and beliefs.

When you show consistent commitment to your core message during an interview, you gain recognition for your beliefs and values, which establishes you as a reliable and trustworthy source of information. Maintaining this consistency in your core message, storytelling, and expertise throughout each interview builds a strong foundation of credibility with both the host and their audience. This consistency demonstrates that you are authentic, knowledgeable, and committed to providing valuable content.

Case Study - Commitment and Consistency

A compelling example of the importance of commitment and consistency in podcast interviews features a guest named Michael, a technology consultant specializing in innovative software solutions. Throughout his interviews, Michael highlighted his dedication to three foundational pillars of effective problem-solving: teamwork, innovation, and adaptability. He consistently wove these themes into his responses, reinforcing both his commitment to these principles and his core message.

In each interview, Michael also shared anecdotes from past projects to highlight the value of teamwork. He explained how collaboration led to significant breakthroughs, emphasizing that different perspectives foster robust solutions. This resonated with the audience and solidified Michael's credibility as a thought leader in the tech industry.

By focusing on commitment and consistency, Michael demonstrated that adhering to proven methods and maintaining high standards can lead to sustained success. He pointed out that the consistent application of innovative practices enables businesses to build a strong foundation and achieve long-term growth, even when challenges arise. His unwavering dedication to these principles reinforced the significance of commitment and consistency across all areas of business.

By embodying these values, Michael enhanced his relationship with both the host and the listeners. The host appreciated his clear messaging and expressed interest in inviting Michael back for future discussions, recommending him to other networks and leading to further opportunities.

Social Proof

Up next is Cialdini's principle of social proof, a powerful psychological concept that's highly relevant for your podcast interviews. Social proof suggests that people tend to adopt certain behaviors or beliefs when they observe others, particularly those they trust or admire, doing the same. By leveraging social proof in your interviews, you can enhance your credibility, influence listener perceptions, and ultimately boost your podcast marketing results.

Utilizing social proof before a podcast interview involves demonstrating your expertise, authority, and credibility to the host. You can highlight your past achievements, industry recognition, and positive feedback from previous interviews. By providing evidence of your knowledge and experience, you create social proof that strengthens your reputation as a trusted expert in your field. This proactive approach can capture the host's interest, enhance your chances of being selected for an interview, and foster a positive atmosphere for the upcoming conversation.

Social proof is crucial during your interview. You can boost your credibility by mentioning endorsements, testimonials, or support from industry leaders and satisfied customers. Sharing relevant success stories, case studies, or statistics can further validate your insights and recommendations. By incorporating social proof into the conversation, you can enhance your persuasiveness, build rapport with the host and their audience, and create connections through shared experiences or endorsements from credible sources.

Social proof is also crucial after an interview because it can amplify the impact of your discussion and extend your reach. You can leverage social proof by sharing snippets or highlights from the interview on social media, collecting website testimonials, or submitting to industry publications. Encouraging listeners to leave positive reviews, testimonials, or comments about your interview can enhance your social proof and attract new audiences to engage with your content. Additionally, collaborating with the host to promote your interview and cross-promoting on each other's channels can further strengthen social proof and bolster your credibility.

Case Study - Social Proof

In this example, Emma, who recently launched her handmade jewelry business, faced challenges in attracting customers to her online store. Recognizing the power of Robert Cialdini's Social Proof principle, she turned to podcast marketing to promote her brand while showcasing testimonials and reviews from her initial customers. After making guest appearances on craft and entrepreneurship podcasts, Emma encouraged her early buyers to share their experiences on these platforms, emphasizing their appreciation for the unique designs and quality of her pieces. Positive endorsements from buyers created trust and validation for potential customers, boosting their confidence in making a purchase.

Emma further enhanced her strategy by incorporating feedback and testimonials into her podcast discussions. She shared stories about how her jewelry positively impacted customers' lives, making the content relatable and engaging for listeners. Additionally, Emma used her social media channels to highlight photos of happy customers wearing her jewelry, encouraging them to tag her with a dedicated hashtag. This fostered a sense of community around her brand and prompted others to share their own experiences.

As a result of implementing these social proof strategies through podcast appearances and social media, Emma experienced a significant increase in sales and customer inquiries. New customers were eager to buy her jewelry, reassured by the positive experiences of others. By effectively leveraging the Social Proof principle, Emma transformed her business into a trusted brand, building credibility and ultimately driving sustainable growth along with an expanding customer base through the power of community endorsement.

Authority

To illustrate the power of Cialdini's next principle, authority, think about a favorite teacher at school who always knows the answers and explains things clearly. You trust their advice and see them as an expert in their subject. This shows the influence of authority—when we naturally respect and follow the guidance of someone we view as knowledgeable or experienced in a particular area.

Authority is like having a guide or mentor who helps you navigate uncertainties. It involves seeking individuals with expertise, credibility, or status to assist in our decisions because we trust their knowledge can lead us in the right direction. For example, if a lawyer recommends a particular course of action to achieve a specific legal outcome, you're likely to follow their advice because you view lawyers as authorities. Similarly, if a renowned scientist explains how an experiment works, you're more inclined to trust their explanation due to their expertise in the field.

In everyday life, we encounter authority when we adhere to rules set by teachers or parents since we believe they know what's best for us. This is also why we may trust the advice of a guest expert on a podcast about improving skills in which they already excel.

Understanding the authority principle shows that, as a guest, you have the power to influence the audience as a leader in your field. Being aware of this can enhance the credibility of the information you present in each interview, enabling listeners to make more informed decisions about you and your business. It's vital to leverage the power of your authority to shape the audience's beliefs and actions, guiding them toward your solutions.

Case Study - Authority

In this example, James, a fitness coach, decided to launch an online program to promote healthy living and personalized workout routines. To establish his credibility, James showcased his background, including his certifications, years of experience, and success stories from previous clients on his website and social media platforms. By presenting himself as an authority in fitness, he instilled confidence in potential clients regarding his ability to guide them in achieving their health goals.

To further reinforce his authority, James collaborated with well-known health experts, nutritionists, and fitness influencers, inviting them to participate in his online content. These featured guests endorsed his program, shared their expertise, and highlighted the effectiveness of James's coaching methods. Their involvement not only increased the perceived value of his offerings but also attracted a broader audience interested in fitness and health, as people are more likely to follow recommendations from established authorities in the field.

As a result of applying the Authority principle, James's online program quickly gained traction. Testimonials from satisfied clients, expert endorsements, and informative content positioned him as a trusted resource in the fitness industry. This increased authority helped him attract more clients, boost sales for his program, and build a loyal community, demonstrating that establishing authority could significantly enhance his business and impact in the health and fitness space.

Liking

Robert Cialdini's principle of liking is much like making friends. Imagine meeting someone new at school who shares your interests, laughs at your jokes, and is enjoyable to be around. You start to like them more because of the connection you feel, based on shared interests and positive interactions.

Liking involves how we naturally feel closer to people who are similar to us, who compliment us, or with whom we enjoy spending time. It's akin to finding a podcast guest who aligns with your interests; you instantly feel that connection. This principle is effective because we are more likely to agree to the requests of people we know, like, and trust.

Think about your favorite teacher who makes learning enjoyable or your best friend who always supports you. You are more inclined to respond positively to their requests because of your positive relationship with them. In daily life, liking influences our choices about which friends to spend time with, which celebrities to admire, and which brands to prefer. We are attracted to people and things that make us feel good, valued, or understood.

To apply the liking principle in your interviews, it's essential to build rapport and show genuine interest in others. By being friendly, helpful, and authentic, you create connections that encourage people to listen to you and be more willing to agree to your requests to subscribe, visit your website, or check out your solution.

Case Study - Liking

In this example, allow me to introduce Jack, a 25-year-old startup software developer. Imagine you, a fellow software enthusiast, discovering Jack in a podcast interview. You notice that Jack shares more than just software tricks and tips; his conversation is filled with humor, captivating stories, and a genuine passion for software that shines through in every part of the discussion.

As you listen to Jack's interview, you are drawn not only to the software advice but also to his friendly and relatable personality. He shares personal anecdotes, tells jokes, and interacts with listeners, making you feel like you're part of a genuine software community.

You start to see Jack not just as a skilled developer but also as a friend. You admire his authenticity, humor, and the way he treats his listeners like friends hanging out together. The more interviews you listen to, the stronger your connection with Jack becomes.

One day, Jack announces a meet-up event for software developers in his local area. Excited about the chance to meet your podcast hero in person, you agree to join him. At the event, you find that Jack is just as friendly and approachable in real life as he is during his podcast interviews. You chat about software and even receive a few personalized tips from Jack himself.

Through the likability principle, your admiration for Jack grows not only because of his software skills but also because of the likable and relatable person he is during his podcast interviews. This connection leads you to become a loyal listener and fan who eagerly anticipates each new interview with Jack.

Scarcity

Scarcity, as explained by Cialdini, happens when the latest popular mobile phone is almost sold out or when your favorite snack is available for a limited time. This concept shows that items become more attractive when there is a limited supply or a deadline. When you see something as rare or likely to go away soon, your desire for it grows.

Scarcity is powerful because it creates a sense of urgency and motivates us to act before we lose an opportunity. This principle applies when you present your solution to your interview listeners in limited quantities, prompting them to rush to buy one out of fear of missing out. So, near the end of each interview, encourage listeners to act before your special offer expires.

To implement the scarcity principle in your interviews, highlight the unique features or limited availability of your solution to enhance its appeal. By showing that it's in short supply or won't be available for long, you create a sense of FOMO—fear of missing out—that encourages listeners to act quickly.

Scarcity involves instilling a sense of rarity and urgency to make your solution more attractive and desirable. By understanding and applying this principle during your interviews, you can boost the perceived value of your offer and motivate others to take action before it's too late.

Case Study - Scarcity

Imagine Dave, a 30-year-old business owner who loves the podcast "Business Builders." The show features the host, a successful business owner, interviewing various professionals to discuss different business topics. One day, Dave discovers that the podcast is set to release a limited interview series comprising just five episodes, each focused on sharing key insights that can significantly impact his business.

Excited about the announcement, Dave sets a reminder for the launch date. As the release date approaches, the podcast team begins a countdown on social media to build anticipation. Dave notices that other listeners are also eager about the limited interview series, sharing their excitement online.

When the first episode finally airs, Dave is hooked. The content is relevant and highly helpful, and its practical impact on his business is clear. The podcast host emphasizes that this is a one-time series with no reruns or extended releases.

Feeling the urgency of the limited release, Dave eagerly listens to each episode, trying to piece together the information before the final tip is revealed at the end of the series. The scarcity of each episode enhances his listening experience, knowing that once the series concludes, it will remain unique and exclusive to those who participated, never to be available again.

By using the scarcity principle during your interviews, you can help listeners appreciate each episode even more. This simple yet powerful approach fosters a sense of FOMO (fear of missing out) and adds special appeal to your limited interview content.

Unity

Robert Cialdini's unity principle is akin to being part of a team where everyone feels connected by a common goal. It suggests that we are more likely to agree with or support those who are similar to us or belong to the same group. Unity emphasizes the sense of togetherness and shared identity, which fosters closeness and influences our decisions.

For instance, imagine you're at a school event where students from various classes come together to support their sports team. Even if they don't know each other well, they all cheer for their team and they all want it to win. This sense of unity creates a bond among them, making them more likely to support one another.

Cialdini's unity principle is crucial in your podcast appearances because it harnesses the power of shared identities and connections that shape your audience's behavior. Listeners are more inclined to trust and cooperate with you when they see you as part of their "in-group" or as someone who shares similar traits or beliefs.

Unity plays a significant role in the success of your interview campaign because it appeals to our natural tendency to support those we perceive as part of our tribe or community. For example, meeting someone who shares your taste in movies or music creates an instant connection, making it easier to bond with them.

To apply the unity principle effectively during your interviews, emphasize shared identity, experiences, or values to cultivate a sense of belonging and rapport. By highlighting commonalities and fostering feelings of unity, you will build trust, strengthen your relationship with the audience, and encourage them to take action.

Case Study - Unity

In this example, Lisa, the owner of a popular coffee shop, recognized that fostering a sense of community was crucial for attracting and retaining customers. Inspired by Robert Cialdini's Unity principle, she enhanced her marketing efforts by incorporating podcast appearances to promote her coffee shop. During her interviews, Lisa highlighted the culture of her shop, sharing stories about sourcing beans, the art of brewing, and the joy of bringing people together over a cup of coffee.

To further promote unity among her customers, Lisa began hosting weekly coffee tasting events that encouraged attendees to share their experiences and learn about different brews. She promoted these events through in-store signage, social media, and her podcast interviews, inviting listeners to join the community and bond over their shared love for coffee. By effectively using podcast marketing, she reached a wider audience and positioned her coffee shop as a welcoming space where everyone felt they belonged.

Additionally, Lisa introduced a "Coffee Club" loyalty program that rewarded regular customers for their patronage. Members who joined through promotions mentioned in her podcast received exclusive perks, such as discounts, early access to new blends, and invitations to members-only events. By emphasizing shared interests and providing ways for customers to get involved, Lisa cultivated a strong sense of identity among club members, making them feel valued in a community dedicated to coffee appreciation.

As a result of implementing the Unity principle through podcast marketing, Lisa saw a noticeable increase in customer loyalty and community engagement. Customers became passionate advocates for the shop, frequently sharing their experiences on social media and inviting friends to tasting events. This sense of belonging not only enhanced customer satisfaction but also established Lisa's coffee shop as a beloved gathering spot in the neighborhood, demonstrating the profound impact of unity in community building and effective marketing.

Unique Value Proposition

In a saturated market, it's easy for your business to get lost amid the competition, making it difficult to attract quality customers. This is where a unique value proposition becomes essential. By highlighting the distinct benefits, value, and solutions your business offers during interviews and on landing pages, you can stand out, capture the attention of your ideal prospects, and convert them into paying customers.

For your podcast marketing system to succeed, you need to identify your unique selling points. These are the specific features, qualities, or benefits that differentiate your products or services from the competition. Take the time to analyze what makes your offerings unique, considering aspects such as quality, innovation, convenience, price, customer service, or any other element that sets you apart.

For example, if you're a software company, your unique selling points might include a user-friendly interface, advanced features, seamless integration with other platforms, or exceptional customer support. If you're a service-based business, your unique selling points could be specialized expertise, personalized attention, or a distinctive approach to problem-solving.

Once you've identified and crafted your unique selling points, share them with your target audience and existing customers to see if they resonate with them before discussing them during an interview or posting them on your landing page. Ask for your audience's opinions, suggestions, and any improvements they may have before formally adding them to your podcast marketing strategy. Based on the feedback you receive, refine and iterate your value proposition until you achieve the right balance, and continue to review your selling points to ensure they remain relevant.

After testing the efficacy of your unique selling points, what you say about them during your next interview will set your business apart from the competition. By investing time to define your selling points, you'll be offering something your competitors don't. In many cases, this is enough for listeners to choose your solution over others.

To determine your unique selling points, document everything you know about your ideal customer. What makes you and your business unique compared to your competition, and how can you explain this effectively during an interview? How will listeners recognize that what you offer is right for them, and what benefits will distinguish you from your competitors?

Before you introduce your unique value proposition during an interview, you first need to clearly understand the core problem and then articulate your questions conversationally. When you understand what your ideal customer wants and communicate in a language they understand, you're more likely to connect with them in a way that leads to a purchasing decision.

Target Audience

Understanding your target audience, buyer types, and buyer personas is essential for maximizing the impact of your podcast guest interviews. These concepts serve as the foundation for your podcast marketing strategy, enabling you to tailor your content and messaging to meet the specific needs, interests, and preferences of your listeners.

Target Audience: Your target audience is the specific group of people you want to reach with your podcast interviews. Identifying this audience helps you choose relevant topics and select appropriate shows that align with your expertise and interests. By understanding who your listeners are—including their age, gender, profession, and hobbies—you can create content that directly addresses their challenges and aspirations. This focused approach enhances listener engagement and fosters a deeper connection between you and your audience.

Buyer Types: Recognizing the different buyer types within your audience is crucial for influencing their purchasing decisions. For instance, some listeners may be analytical, relying on data and facts to make informed choices, while others may be more impulsive, driven by emotions and the desire for instant gratification. By understanding these buyer types, you can tailor your interview content to address the diverse motivations of your audience. This includes providing data-driven insights for analytical listeners, engaging stories for impulsive buyers, and reassurance for those who are skeptical.

Buyer Personas: A buyer persona is a semi-fictional representation of your ideal listener, created from market research and real customer data. Developing detailed buyer personas involves identifying the specific challenges, motivations, and behaviors of your target audience. This understanding allows you to craft compelling narratives and engage in relevant discussions during your podcast interviews. When you know who you are speaking to, you can respond to targeted questions, provide valuable insights, and position yourself as a trusted authority for your listeners.

Involve The Audience

Involving your target audience before, during, and after each interview is crucial for achieving your podcast marketing goals. To this end, focus on connecting, sharing your message, and building relationships with listeners across relevant platforms throughout the interview process. By prioritizing your audience's needs, you can create meaningful experiences that add value and encourage listeners to learn more about your business.

The following pages provide insight into various strategies for capturing the attention of your target audience before, during, and after each interview. This approach will naturally attract them to your business, book, or venture, encouraging them to self-select and seek out more information.

Involve The Audience - BTI

Enticing Subscribers with Exclusive Insights

Email newsletters are an effective way to nurture your audience and keep them informed about upcoming interviews. By sending exclusive sneak peeks, bonus content, or personalized messages, you make subscribers feel valued and encourage their engagement. Offering early access to interview recordings, special discounts, or additional resources related to the discussion can motivate subscribers to stay connected and look forward to your content.

Gathering Feedback Through Audience Polls

Conducting audience polls is another effective way to gather insights and preferences before an interview. Use polls to discover which topics resonate most with your audience, what they expect from your interviews, and any specific questions they want you to address. Adjusting your content based on audience feedback demonstrates that you value their opinions and helps keep your interviews relevant and engaging.

Building Anticipation with Virtual Events

Organizing virtual events like live Q&A sessions or webinars before an interview is a fantastic way to foster community and excitement. These events allow you to preview key discussion points, introduce yourself, and enable listeners to interact by asking questions or sharing their thoughts. Hosting interactive sessions adds a personal touch to your engagement strategy and helps the audience connect with the upcoming interview in a dynamic manner.

Involve The Audience - DTI

Storytelling Techniques: Incorporating storytelling techniques into your podcast interview can captivate listeners and boost engagement. Use anecdotes, personal experiences, or case studies to illustrate key points, making your information relatable and memorable. Engaging storytelling not only educates but also entertains, creating a lasting impact on the audience.

Interactive Segments: Incorporating interactive segments, such as audience questions or polls, encourages participation during the interview. For instance, when live streaming an interview, consider adding audience questions or interactive quizzes to increase listener involvement. This engagement strategy fosters a sense of community and shows that you value listener input.

Live Chat Features: Setting up a live chat feature during a live stream interview can significantly enhance listener engagement by providing real-time interaction. This allows listeners to share their thoughts, ask questions, and connect with you during the interview, fostering a sense of community and creating a more immersive experience.

Call-to-Action Prompts: Incorporating call-to-action (CTA) prompts during your interview encourages listeners to take specific actions afterward. Whether directing them to visit your website, subscribe to your newsletter, or download additional resources, clear and compelling CTAs guide listeners on how to engage with your business.

Involve The Audience - ATI

Continue The Conversation With Email: After your interview, sending personalized follow up emails can further boost engagement. Thank the host, share the interview link, and offer additional resources related to the topics discussed. Including exclusive content or relevant articles can keep your audience engaged beyond the interview.

Podcast Recap Blogs: Creating podcast recap blogs can effectively summarize key points and insights from your interviews. These blogs extend the conversation, providing a written overview that highlights key takeaways and memorable quotes. Recap blogs also increase content discoverability and encourage further discussion among your audience.

Social Media Campaigns: Utilizing social media to share highlights and key takeaways from your interview amplifies reach and sparks conversations. Create visually appealing posts featuring snippets or quotes from the interview to grab attention and invite engagement.

Community Building: Establishing a dedicated community for listeners to connect, discuss previous interviews, and share thoughts fosters a sense of belonging. Consider creating an online forum or group for ongoing engagement centered on your content.

Leverage AI Tools: AI tools offer exciting opportunities to enhance audience engagement through personalized interactions. For example, AI-powered chatbots can provide real-time responses to inquiries, recommend content, and present tailored promotions, creating more meaningful interactions.

Expand Reach with Voice-Activated Devices: The rise of voice-activated devices presents a unique opportunity to engage audiences through voice-based interactions. Optimizing content for voice search and creating interactive voice experiences can help you reach a broader audience.

Enhance the Experience with Virtual Assistants: Integrating virtual assistants into your promotional efforts allows you to provide instant support and personalized recommendations, resulting in a more engaging listening experience.

By combining traditional and innovative attention-grabbing techniques outlined in this section, you can forge stronger connections with your audience, encourage community interaction, and drive meaningful conversations. Embracing these approaches will not only improve your audience's interview experience but also open up opportunities for sustained growth, increased reach, and greater overall impact.

Case Study - Involve The Audience

During an interview on "The Business Builders Podcast," guest Simon Smith used various strategies to captivate listeners. He began by sharing a personal story about his business challenges and how someone he met inspired him to make critical changes that turned his struggling business around. This hook immediately resonated with listeners facing similar struggles.

Throughout the interview, the host encouraged Simon to elaborate on the changes he made and to explain why they were effective. This conversational approach led to rich discussions and valuable insights that connected with Simon's target audience.

In one particularly informative segment, Simon answered listener questions submitted via social media prior to the interview. This interactive portion not only captured listeners' attention but also made them feel valued, as Simon addressed their specific concerns and queries.

The combination of a strong hook, open-ended questions, storytelling, and audience feedback significantly enhanced the interview. As a result, there was a notable increase in listener downloads and social media mentions, highlighting the importance of audience involvement.

Power of Social Media

Social media plays a crucial role in raising awareness about your upcoming interviews. By effectively using platforms like Instagram, X, and Facebook, you can create a compelling narrative around your content. Begin by crafting engaging posts that tease topics to be explored, share behind-the-scenes glimpses, or pose thought-provoking questions related to the discussion.

When preparing for an interview, consider sharing a striking photo of your workspace or a short video discussing a pivotal moment in your career. You might ask, "What innovation do you think changed the game in [your industry]?" Such posts invite followers to engage and generate excitement for the upcoming interview. Encouraging your audience to share their thoughts or questions can further involve them in the discussion, even if it is pre-recorded, increasing the likelihood that they will tune in.

Incorporating interactive elements like polls or contests can significantly boost engagement. For instance, you could host a poll asking your audience to vote on which aspect of your entrepreneurial journey they find most intriguing: "Would you rather hear about your biggest failure or your most significant breakthrough?." These strategies not only spark interest but also empower listeners, making them feel valued in the content creation process.

From a technical standpoint, building anticipation through social media can enhance your reach and visibility. Social media algorithms favor posts that attract attention, leading to broader content distribution. The more interactions your posts attract, the more likely they are to draw in new users, connecting them to you and your business.

Podcast Marketing Funnel

I recently read "Ready, Fire, Aim" by Michael Masterson. In this renowned business-building book, Masterson discusses the four stages of entrepreneurial growth and outlines the essential skills for success. He also emphasizes the most critical aspect of any entrepreneurial venture: marketing.

This section will help you create your own podcast marketing funnel to guide listeners from your interviews into your marketing process. Your interviews will attract interested listeners who will then become leads. You will nurture these leads until they either exit your funnel or purchase your solution.

Having your own unique podcast marketing funnel consisting of a number of connected steps will guide your ideal prospects from initial awareness through to purchase. When creating your podcast marketing funnel, prioritize simplicity and ease of use by establishing a smooth process that takes listeners through each stage of your promotional funnel.

Typically, a promotional funnel has six stages that a prospect goes through before making a purchasing decision. These stages include awareness, interest, consideration, intent, evaluation, and purchase. Your goal is to guide interested listeners through each stage, nurturing them along the way and ultimately converting them into customers.

Importantly, consider what you want from your marketing funnel before starting your interview journey. Each stage of your funnel should be carefully planned and aligned with the specific topics of your guest interviews. Your funnel must guide each prospect toward the product or service you want them to discover.

In the awareness stage of your funnel, focus on building brand recognition and capturing the attention of your target audience. During this phase, promote your interviews on social media, your website, and, if applicable, to your email list. Additionally, share snippets that tease your upcoming interviews to draw in more interest.

Once you've captured your audience's attention, the next step is the interest stage. Your goal here is to provide valuable content that deepens their interest, engages them, and addresses their specific pain points. To this end, during each interview, offer in-depth discussions, expert insights, and useful knowledge that resonate with your audience's specific needs and challenges.

During an interview, engaged listeners will start to consider if your offer can solve their problems or meet their needs. So, it's essential to highlight the benefits of your products and services or refer them to other interviews where you've discussed these advantages.

To help listeners who want to learn more, provide clear and easy-to-follow instructions. At this stage, your goal is to convert listeners into leads. You can do this by including a compelling call to-action towards the end of each interview. For example, you might say, "Hey, thanks for having me on your show! If your listeners want to learn more, they can visit my website at [add your landing page URL]." Make sure your call-to-action is clear and engaging enough for your target audience to think, "Hey, that's for me."

When an interested listener takes action and follows your instructions, they will evaluate your offer against other options. At this stage, it's essential to share reviews, testimonials, success stories, and other positive feedback about your solution to build trust and credibility with your prospect. You can do this by either sharing relevant success stories during the conversation or by adding them to your landing page.

Lastly, once a prospect has gone through each of the stages described, they'll be ready to either exit your funnel or make a purchase. To encourage a buying decision, enhance your offer by including special discounts or limited-time offers exclusively for interview listeners. Make sure to highlight these on the page where you direct them.

"***The one function that should be given top priority in an entrepreneurial venture is marketing***" **- Michael Masterson**

Case Study - Podcast Marketing Funnel

Andrew, a dedicated financial coach, used his podcast guest appearances to expand his reach and share his expertise. He selected personal finance podcasts aimed at aspiring investors and secured several guest spots. By promoting these interviews on platforms like LinkedIn and X, he generated buzz and increased awareness of his insights and expertise.

During his appearance on the "Monopoly Money Matters Podcast," Andrew captivated listeners by sharing his journey from debt to financial independence. He included relatable anecdotes and practical investing tips. As the host encouraged listeners to visit Andrew's website for additional resources, interest in his solutions surged and has remained steady since the interview.

To capitalize on this, Andrew provided a free downloadable guide titled "5 Essential Steps to Financial Freedom," which not only delivered value but also captured email addresses to grow his subscriber list. His interviews included clear calls-to-action, prompting listeners to check out his online financial coaching program. Following the interview, Andrew sent welcome emails filled with financial tips and exclusive discounts, fostering deeper connections with his audience.

As his community grew, satisfied clients shared their positive experiences, promoting Andrew's podcast appearances on social media. This organic advocacy strengthened his reputation as a trusted authority in the financial coaching arena. Through effective engagement at each stage of the podcast marketing funnel, Andrew successfully transformed listeners into loyal customers and advocates for his brand.

Own Your Online Real Estate

James Schramko, a well-known online business coach and entrepreneur, often uses the metaphor of "owning the racecourse" to describe a strategic approach to business and marketing. This concept emphasizes the importance of controlling your own platforms and assets, such as your website, email list, and customer relationships, rather than relying solely on third-party platforms like social media.

By "owning the racecourse," Schramko advocates for creating a business model where you have direct access to your audience and can engage with them on your terms. This approach allows for greater stability, control over your messaging, and the ability to build long-term relationships with customers. It also mitigates risks associated with changes in third-party platforms, such as algorithm updates or policy changes that could impact your reach and engagement.

Although creating a free account on social media platforms can be appealing for those who prefer not to manage their own website, you don't own or control these platforms. If Facebook, YouTube, or any other platform finds your content unsuitable, you risk losing the ability to connect with your audience.

Imagine that you were using a free social media platform, and your account was suddenly closed without warning or explanation. Without an online presence, how will listeners learn about your products and services after each interview?

If you don't have an online presence that you control, like a website or landing page, and people can't find your business through a simple search or clickable link, you'll be at a competitive disadvantage, making your interview strategy largely ineffective.

Yes, if your audience is on social media, definitely promote your upcoming and existing interviews on those platforms. However, always own and maintain your own online space. Be sure to mention how people can find you during your interviews and encourage listeners to visit your website or landing page after the interview ends.

The key takeaway is that free social media platforms are not digital real estate you own. If you don’t control your online presence, it can be taken away. To prevent this, create your own online real estate where your audience can connect, download your lead magnet, learn more about your business, and make purchases.

Having your own online real estate, whether it's a website or landing page, is crucial for maximizing the impact of your interviews and turning interested listeners into engaged followers, customers, and clients. Your online space adds credibility and legitimacy while showcasing your background, achievements, and solutions. It can also serve as a platform for additional resources such as blog posts and videos, as well as a way to download free materials that further educate and engage your audience.

Another important reason to have your own online real estate is that there's no guarantee that previous hosts and their platforms will keep your interviews available now or in the future. Their show might go offline permanently, or they may decide to remove your interview, leaving your target audience without access to your content.

With this in mind, it's essential to have an agreement with each host to obtain a copy of your interview, whether it's in audio or video format. Additionally, make sure you establish the right to use your copy of the interview on your own platforms without any restrictions.

"*Own The Racecourse*"

- James Schramko

The Power of WordPress

One way to create an online space you control is by building your own website. During my research, I discovered an article about a platform called WordPress. After reading it, I couldn't stop thinking about how I could use WordPress to promote my business. This curiosity led me to learn everything I could about the platform. Before long, I was ready to create my own website, and within a few weeks, I had launched the first version of my online real estate.

For your podcast marketing strategy to be effective, it's important to have a space where interested listeners can learn more about your products and services. The platform you choose is crucial for your podcast marketing funnel. Based on my experience, while there are many options available, I believe WordPress can be a key asset in your podcast marketing strategy, as it can serve as individual landing pages or a complete website.

To emphasize the importance of having your own online real estate, picture this: you share your interviews on different platforms, only to face rejection, removal, or deletion. The unfortunate reality of relying on platforms you don't own is that they hold the power. They can make choices that benefit them, and there's little you can do to stop them from taking down your content.

Thanks to WordPress, you can establish a permanent home for your interview content that cannot be removed or deleted, making your website the central hub of your business. It serves as a space where visitors can learn more, access your special offers, and become buyers of your products and services.

Landing Pages

There's no point in giving interviews unless you can turn a listener into a lead, and then a lead into a customer. So, come to each interview prepared with a link to a landing page specifically designed for the show's audience.

While many people will listen to your interview and want to learn more, even after becoming a lead, most won't be ready to make a purchase. This is why interviews serve to introduce yourself, educate your audience, raise awareness of the solutions you offer, and encourage listeners to visit a landing page designed specifically for them.

Landing pages are a vital part of your podcast marketing funnel because they provide extra information about your business, book, or project. When listeners finish your interview and want to learn more, they visit your landing page, share their contact information, and enter your funnel. From there, you can build the relationship by offering additional value through emails and different types of content until those leads turn into customers.

The main goal of a landing page is to collect contact details from interested listeners. These individuals have demonstrated interest in your content and the solutions your business offers. They've listened to your interview, followed your instructions, shared their contact information, and are positioned to learn more about your core offer.

When creating a landing page that leads to your core offer, add an attention-grabbing headline and sub-headline. As you craft the headline, think about the fears and frustrations your ideal prospect experiences, and choose words that resonate with them. Write as if you're having a conversation with a friend, expressing genuine excitement about your solution.

Use your landing page to share relevant information, capture contact details, and remind visitors of the page's purpose by referencing your interview. Maintain consistent branding, include testimonials and case studies whenever possible, and ensure your message clearly addresses any potential objections related to your offer.

Every landing page you create must relate to your interview topic. By aligning each landing page with the specific interview topic, you ensure a smooth and familiar experience for visitors. When someone views your landing page, it's essential to present a call to action and an offer. Your offer can be a PDF, a short video, an audio file, or any format that resonates best with your audience.

Importantly, avoid making your landing page too flashy. All visitors want to know is what's in it for them. A simple layout can be divided into three parts: the first part includes the headline and subheading, the middle section features the body copy and testimonials, and the final part presents your offer, guarantees and a final call-to-action.

Over time, you will develop a series of landing pages related to the subjects discussed in each interview. At the end of each interview, let listeners know where they can find more information and provide a link to the relevant landing page.

To capture email addresses, prominently position an email opt-in form on your landing page. This will help collect email addresses from visitors who come after listening to your interview. Include relevant information about the interview and a message reminding visitors of the interview while encouraging them to access your opt-in offer.

To guide listeners to your landing pages, include a clear call-to-action at the end of each interview. Always ask listeners to visit your landing page and take action, such as subscribing to your email list. When creating a landing page specific to your interview, use a memorable URL that includes the podcast name where you appeared, making it easier for listeners to find your page.

Landing Pages - Good vs Bad

In this example, consider Tom, an eCommerce entrepreneur who frequently appears on various business and marketing podcasts to showcase his expertise. After each interview, Tom directs listeners to his dedicated landing page, specifically designed to convert podcast audiences into leads.

Tom's landing page is thoughtfully crafted to maximize leads. At the top, it features a captivating headline: "Unlock Exclusive Discounts on the Latest Trends!" The subheading emphasizes what sets him apart: "Join thousands who shop with confidence and style." Below this, eye-catching visuals display his best-selling products, creating an immediate connection with potential buyers. The page includes a lead magnet: a free downloadable guide, "Top 10 Must-Have Products," which visitors can access by entering their email addresses. The prominently placed call-to-action button, brightly colored, reads "Claim Your Free Guide!" inviting immediate action.

In contrast, consider Mark, another podcast guest whose landing page is ineffective. His page opens with a generic headline, "Welcome to My Store Page," which fails to present any enticing offer or connection to visitors. Instead of engaging visuals, the page is cluttered with dense blocks of text, making it overwhelming for users. There is no lead magnet or incentive for listeners to provide their email information, leading to a lack of engagement. Additionally, the absence of testimonials diminishes Mark's credibility, leaving potential customers uncertain about the quality and reliability of his products.

The difference between Tom’s well-structured landing page and Mark's poorly designed one is significant. Tom’s page successfully captures attention and presents a clear, attractive offer, thus increasing the likelihood of conversion. In contrast, Mark’s landing page fails to connect with its audience, missing essential elements required to inspire action, such as clear value propositions, appealing content, and social proof.

Lead Magnets

Having a landing page without a lead magnet is like hosting a treasure hunt without treasure— there's nothing to entice people to share their contact information. Just as treasures create excitement during a treasure hunt, a lead magnet is essential for attracting visitors to your landing page. In short, without a valuable free offer or incentive, visitors are less likely to provide their contact details.

Use your lead magnet as an "invitation" to attract and engage your target audience. This encourages them to take a desired action, such as signing up for a newsletter, downloading a resource, or making a purchase. Providing a compelling and relevant lead magnet in exchange for their name and email on a landing page is the first step in building a mutually beneficial relationship with your potential customers.

When paired with a landing page, a well-designed lead magnet will collect listener information in exchange for free content that addresses a single problem. It's important to emphasize that gathering each visitor's name and email address is crucial for growing your business using this podcast marketing strategy.

By providing access to valuable content or resources in exchange for a visitor's email address, you can build a list of engaged and interested prospects. You can then nurture these leads through email marketing campaigns and other promotional activities, ultimately leading to sales and sustainable business growth.

For example, you could create a cheat sheet that covers a specific topic related to your expertise. If you were a guest on a podcast discussing financial planning for entrepreneurs, you might offer a cheat sheet titled "The Ultimate Cheat Sheet to Financial Planning for Small Business Owners." The key to any offer is to ensure that it's high-quality and provides actionable advice that people can implement immediately.

Your cheat sheet or checklist could summarize the key points from your podcast interview. This can serve as a quick reference guide for listeners to implement the advice or strategies you shared during the interview. For instance, if you were a guest on a podcast about time management for busy professionals, you could provide a checklist called "10 Time-Saving Strategies for Maximizing Productivity."

Alternatively, you could create an introductory video or audio training that offers guidance on a specific topic related to your solution. This could be a step-by-step tutorial or a series of short lessons that help listeners explore the concepts you discussed in your interview. For instance, if you were a guest on a podcast discussing social media marketing, you might provide a video training session titled "Mastering Social Media: A Comprehensive Guide to Building Your Online Presence."

Now that you have some inspiration from the examples, it's time to create your own compelling lead magnet. Before you start, it's important to understand your target audience and their specific needs and pain points. What challenges do they face, and what solutions can you offer? By identifying the problems your audience encounters and how you can address them, you can create a lead magnet that truly resonates with them.

Your lead magnet must provide real value to your audience. It should address a specific problem or offer a solution that they can implement right away. Avoid offering generic lead magnets that don't deliver on their promises. The more relevant, valuable, and actionable your offer is, the more likely listeners will be to share their contact information.

Additionally, while it's crucial to provide relevant value upfront, people are often busy. Ensure that your lead magnet is easy to understand and consume. Break down complex concepts into simple steps, and use clear, straightforward language that is easy to follow and implement.

Visual elements can significantly enhance the appeal of your lead magnet. Use images, graphics, and colors that align with your brand to create an attractive design. Visuals not only make your offer more appealing but also help communicate complex information quickly and effectively.

Keep in mind that many internet users access content on mobile devices. Therefore, it's essential to optimize your lead magnet for mobile viewing. Make sure your offer is suitable for mobile readers and verify that it displays correctly on various screen sizes.

One of the most important aspects of your lead magnet is to include a clear and compelling call-to-action that encourages listeners to take the next step. Use actionable language and clearly outline the steps they need to follow to access your core offer.

***"The best lead magnet fulfills a valuable need of your audience and positions you as an expert and trusted resource in your industry."* - Neil Patel**

Podcast Marketing Triangle

To deploy your podcast marketing system, you'll use a combination of guest interviews, written content, and videos to create a range of promotional materials, which I refer to as the "podcast marketing triangle."

The first arm of the triangle is always podcast interviews. Interviews are excellent for building a loyal and engaged listener base. They are easy to produce and edit, cost-effective, and require only a basic microphone and a computer with free recording software like Audacity, GarageBand for Mac, or OBS Studio for Windows.

The second arm of your podcast marketing triangle is written posts. I recommend them because they are easy to create and beneficial for search engine optimization. When someone searches for a topic you've discussed and written about, your content is more likely to show up in the search results. Each time you record an interview, a post is created that includes keywords related to that specific topic. These posts are easy to skim for relevant information and can serve as dedicated landing pages for visitors.

The third component of your podcast marketing triangle is video. YouTube lets you upload your videos online for free. You can promote your business, book, or project directly on the platform and use the embedding feature to include videos in your posts. Additionally, you can share your videos on major social media platforms.

Video allows viewers to see and hear your message, showcasing your personality while building trust and authority. When creating video content you will need a high-definition webcam or camera, a computer, editing software, and a good quality microphone.

To get the best results with your podcast marketing system, I recommend implementing every part of the triangle. You don't need to have everything ready right away; you can introduce each element at a pace that works for you. That said, the first part of the triangle is always your podcast interviews.

I recommend recording video interviews because video content is popular and easy to access. By creating video podcast interviews for YouTube, you can reach audiences on the world's second largest search engine. You'll also benefit from built-in keyword features that enhance discoverability and access to analytics to track engagement with your content.

Regardless of the format you choose, your audience values relevant free content. By producing exceptional interview content that emphasizes delivering results without expecting anything in return, and committing fully to this approach, you'll attract the right audience, build goodwill, and inspire action.

Be Prepared

It's always exciting to host amazing guests on my podcast, The My Future Business Show, who are eager to share their knowledge and experiences. Over the years, I've met many talented business owners who have transformed their businesses through podcast interviews.

If you're a business owner, author, or someone with a message to share, preparation is essential for success. This includes finding the right show, pitching yourself to the host, and securing your spot as their guest.

During the preparation phase, you will review different podcasts to gain insights about the host and their audience, ensuring that you, your business, book, or venture is a good match. By the end of this section, you will know how to identify a show that suits you perfectly and recognize those that don't align with your topics and goals.

I will also explain how to create an information pack and shortlist shows that are most likely to respond to your content and align with your business goals. Once you have a shortlist of about a dozen podcasts you want to appear on, I'll guide you on how to contact potential hosts, helping you move on to the next stage in their guest selection process.

The Pitch Process

I've always approached everything in my business with a systems mindset. Therefore, it's no surprise that I have developed a straightforward yet effective system for reaching out to hosts. This system prioritizes simplicity because adding complexity to your pitch process decreases the chances of booking interviews on your preferred shows.

Having a straightforward but reliable system for regularly pitching to podcast hosts is essential if you plan to use podcast guest appearances as part of your ongoing marketing strategy. A systematic approach saves time, ensures consistency, maximizes your outreach efforts, and increases your chances of securing guest interviews.

An important part of the process is pitching yourself to the host. Pitching is more than just sending a generic email to every host you can find. When done right, pitching becomes a strategic tool that enables you to reach out to hosts, introduce yourself, and offer to be their next guest. This involves crafting a compelling pitch that highlights your expertise, outlines your value, and shows why you would be an engaging guest for their audience.

To successfully pitch a host, begin by researching and shortlisting at least a dozen podcasts that align with your business and goals. Look for shows that match your expertise, industry, and target audience. Once you've shortlisted these shows, examine each one's format, the topics they cover, and whether their previous guest profiles are similar to yours to assess your fit for the show.

After carefully reviewing each show and their guest profiles, and being satisfied with your selection, contact each host. Making contact can be challenging, as hosts often have busy schedules. Therefore, your goal should be to make interactions as easy as possible. From your initial contact to your final thank-you email, make sure that everything you say and do is relevant, timely, and builds confidence in your ability to deliver value during the interview.

Regardless of whether it's your first email or your last, personalize each communication by addressing the host by name and mentioning their podcast. Introduce yourself, express your interest in appearing on their show, and explain why you would be a valuable guest, emphasizing any relevant expertise or experiences that make you unique.

Your pitch email sequence is crucial for capturing the host's attention and standing out among other potential guests. To create a pitch email that gets noticed, use a subject line that is concise, attention-grabbing, and relevant to the podcast. Avoid generic subject lines like "Interview Request" and opt for something engaging, such as "I'm About To Show [Podcast Name] Listeners How To Sell More Shiny Widgets."

Highlight your expertise, unique selling points, and any relevant accomplishments that make your pitch stand out. Additionally, demonstrate that you've done your research by referencing specific episodes, topics, or guests that resonated with you. This shows the host that you genuinely appreciate their content and understand their audience.

In my experience, hosts appreciate receiving compliments, reviews, and testimonials about their show. In your opening pitch email, mention that you've left a review about a previous guest's interview or about their show, and include a link to that review.

You may also want to highlight that you're offering a valuable bonus for their listeners, such as a book, course, or access to software. Ensure the host knows what you're offering and, if possible, provide them access before the interview. Close your opening pitch email with a polite thank you, express your excitement about the possibility of appearing on their show, include your contact information, and indicate your openness to further discussion, and how you are looking forward to their response.

The Pitch Kit

The process of booking an interview involves several stages, and making it systematic can simplify the task of finding and connecting with hosts. Having your own unique interview pitch kit, complete with all the necessary information about yourself, your business, and your target audience, not only communicates important details clearly and consistently but also reduces the time it takes to book your spot on the right shows.

When you reach out to a host, they won't know much about you, which is why an interview pitch kit that does the initial 'talking' is essential. The best part of having your own kit is that it serves as a template for contacting a stream of potential hosts, making the pitching process much easier.

A well-constructed pitch kit significantly increases your chances of being invited to speak on your preferred shows. By providing hosts with the necessary information about your professional background, experience, accolades, and awards upfront, you equip them with valuable insights to make informed decisions.

Typically, the host will be the first person to review your guest bio. They will be busy, so it's crucial to get straight to the point and avoid including unnecessary information in your pitch kit that won't aid their decision-making process.

When preparing your pitch kit, apply the 80/20 rule: focus 80% on the value you will add and how it will benefit the audience, and the remaining 20% on details about you and your business. While the exact proportions may vary, the 80/20 rule serves as a helpful guideline for creating an informative and enticing pitch kit.

Start your kit with a well-written introduction and a detailed bio highlighting your background, expertise, and relevant achievements. This section provides hosts with insights into who you are, what you do, and why you would be a good fit for their show and audience.

Provide a suggested shortlist of questions for the interview, making sure to align them with your goals. Providing relevant questions will not only foster meaningful conversations that offer listeners new insights and solutions but also encourage them to learn more about your solutions.

To create relevant talking points, identify the main message you want to convey during the interview. Think about the key takeaways you want the audience to gain and organize your suggested points logically. Personalize your talking points for each pitch kit you send out.

Research each show's audience and tailor your talking points to resonate with their specific interests and needs. This level of customization demonstrates your commitment to delivering relevant content and shows that you've considered the needs of the show and its audience.

Since you'll be reaching out to numerous hosts, save a template version of your pitch kit. When preparing to contact a new host, save a copy of your pitch page template and rename it using the name of the show you're contacting.

Thoughtful personalization also helps create a connection with the host. Mentioning specific episodes or topics they've discussed on their podcast demonstrates that you've engaged with their content and is likely to attract their attention more than a generic pitch.

When customizing your pitch kit, go the extra mile by outlining how you plan to promote their show and distribute your interview. For example, you might mention creating a dedicated post on your website about the host and their show, sending a broadcast message to your email list, or sharing a social media post that tags the host. Each of these actions highlights your support and interest in appearing on their show, which will enhance your chances of securing an interview.

The next part of your pitch kit includes your accomplishments and credentials. Highlight notable achievements, credentials, and other relevant accolades to build your credibility. This increases the host's confidence in your level of expertise. For instance, include professional credentials, awards, speaking engagements, publications, and any notable projects you've been involved with.

On my own pitch page, which is a dedicated section of the My Future Business Directory website, I provide various media assets, including different logo versions in contrasting colors. I also include a high-quality headshot and links to my previous interviews, which may be highlight reels or full-length YouTube videos.

In addition to providing links to previous appearances, include links to testimonials and reviews from former hosts. This social proof positively impacts the host's decision to invite you on their show. Hearing others share their positive experiences with you builds trust and demonstrates that you have delivered valuable content on other shows.

When it's time to present your pitch kit, remember that many hosts may be hesitant to open PDFs due to concerns about viruses or malware. Instead, consider creating an online pitch kit page for your guest bio, which provides a dedicated web link for the host to review. It's good practice to explain why you aren't sending a PDF and invite them to view your online pitch kit.

Finally, ensure that your pitch kit includes a simple way for the host to reach you for further discussion about your appearance. Provide current contact information that allows them to connect via their preferred method of communication, such as email, phone, or website.

If you don't have a website to host your pitch kit page, consider creating a profile on the My Future Business Directory. You can direct potential hosts to your profile page to review your pitch kit information. You'll find a link to set up your pitch kit page in the resources section of this book.

The Pitch Email

Every pitch email should begin with a friendly and engaging introduction that briefly introduces you and your expertise. It should clearly and succinctly explain why you're a suitable guest for their show. Highlight how your expertise or experiences align with the show's theme and target audience, and detail the value you can bring to their show and its listeners. Finally, introduce a selection of potential topics you could discuss that would benefit their audience.

In addition to your opening remarks, showcase relevant accomplishments, publications, or experiences that establish your credibility and demonstrate why you would be an engaging guest. Lastly, include a call to action by politely requesting a guest spot on their show. You might even propose some available recording dates to make it easier for the host to schedule you.

As a host, I've noticed many business owners use Gmail or Hotmail addresses when making initial contact, which often makes me wonder about their business operations. It is always better to use a professional email address instead of a free one for your pitch emails. Additionally, ensure correct spelling and grammar, and maintain a consistent tone throughout each email.

Despite the various channels available for initial contact, email is often the most effective way to make a good first impression when reaching out to hosts. Using email as your primary mode of communication allows you to maintain professionalism, present a detailed pitch, and supply hosts with the necessary information to consider you as a potential guest. Email encourages structured and thoughtful interactions, making it easier for busy hosts to review and respond to your request for an interview.

By leveraging email throughout the pitch process—from the initial pitch to post-interview interactions—you can maintain a professional and organized communication flow with the host. Email not only aids communication but also helps you start building a relationship with the host, showcase your professionalism, and ultimately enhances your reputation as a reliable and sought-after guest.

When creating pitch emails, personalize each message to ensure it resonates with the host, emphasizing how your unique perspective can benefit their audience and add value to their show. By outlining your talking points, showcasing your expertise, and presenting engaging content, you will reduce or eliminate resistance, positioning yourself as a preferred guest candidate.

In every pitch-related email you send, address the host by name to add a personal touch. Remember that the subject line must capture the host's attention; otherwise, your email may go unopened. To give your email the best chance of being opened, create a subject line that briefly summarizes your value proposition, or in other words, what’s in it for the host and their audience.

Example Pitch Email

Subject: Podcast Guest Application: [Your Name] - [Your Expertise/Topic]

Dear [Host's Name],

I hope this email finds you well! My name is [Your Name], and I am a [briefly describe your profession/role, e.g., eCommerce entrepreneur, digital marketing strategist, etc.]. I'm reaching out because I am a big fan of your podcast, [Podcast Name], and I believe that I could offer valuable insights to your audience.

I specialize in [briefly explain your area of expertise or interesting angle related to the podcast's theme, e.g., strategies for successful online selling, the importance of social media marketing, or innovative ways to build customer loyalty]. Having successfully [mention any relevant achievements, such as launching a successful business, writing a bestselling book, etc.], I've gathered insights and experiences that I think would resonate well with your listeners.

I would love the opportunity to discuss [specific topics or themes you'd like to cover in the interview], and share actionable tips that can help your audience navigate the challenges in [specific area related to the podcast's focus]. I can also provide real-life examples and impactful stories that illustrate these points.

Thank you for considering my application! I would be thrilled to contribute to your show and connect with your listeners. Please let me know a convenient time for us to chat or if you would like any further information. Looking forward to hearing from you!

Regards

Follow Up

Podcast hosts are busy individuals who typically manage more than just their podcasts. They have a lot on their minds each day, so it's easy for them to miss important emails.

Following up after your initial pitch email is essential. It keeps you on the host's radar and reinforces your desire to be their guest. Remember, most hosts receive numerous applications, so staying visible increases your chances of being noticed among other applicants.

When you follow up in a timely and respectful manner, you demonstrate your commitment and persistence. You also show the host that you're truly interested in being on their show and that you're willing to put in the effort to make it happen.

For your initial follow-up, wait at least 3-5 business days before sending your next email. This gives hosts enough time to review their emails and consider your pitch before receiving another reminder.

When you do send your follow-up email, wait another 3-5 days before politely inquiring about the status of your pitch. In your follow-up correspondence, express your ongoing interest in being a guest on their show, and offer to provide any additional information if needed.

In many cases, a single follow-up is all it takes to get a response. However, if you don't receive feedback after three follow-ups, consider it a polite decline. If that happens, take a step back and focus your efforts on reaching out to other potential hosts.

Show Selection

Now that you have created a dedicated pitch page and set up your email pitch sequence, it's time to choose the shows that align with you, your business, and your goals. When selecting shows to appear on, it's equally important to avoid shows that are not a good fit. Imagine dedicating time to a show and giving your best interview performance, only to realize you're talking to the wrong audience. Fortunately, you can avoid this by conducting some basic research upfront to identify the right shows for you.

When I was starting in podcasting, I had little knowledge of how the industry operated. It was only after attending a live event and meeting an amazing marketer named Andrew Lock that I discovered podcast interview services. During our conversation, I asked Andrew how he finds shows willing to interview him. He quickly jotted down a link to a podcast booking service called Podcast Guest List. Shortly after registering, I began receiving emails from high-quality podcasts offering interviews.

While Podcast Guest List is a top choice for finding interview-based shows, there are many other platforms that provide information about interview-focused podcasts. Alongside Podcast Guest List, sites like Apple Podcasts, Spotify for Podcasters, Podchaser, Spreaker, TuneIn, YouTube Podcasts, Castbox, Breaker, MatchMaker FM and so on, can all help you find suitable shows.

If you choose to use one of these services, select one and create an account. Ensure your profile is up to date and accurate. Upload a recent headshot and include relevant background information. Most importantly, explain why having you as a guest will add value to their audience. Also, if you provide a link to your website or social media accounts, check that they all work.

As you explore various podcasts, listen to a few episodes of shows that have interviewed guests in your niche. If you find that a show aligns with your topics and goals, features similar guests, and has positive reviews, add it to your shortlist and schedule a time to contact the host with a personalized pitch.

In addition to interview services like Podcast Guest List, you can find shows that align with your interests by conducting a simple Google search with relevant keywords tied to your industry or niche. For instance, if you're in the fitness industry, searching for "fitness podcasts" or "health and wellness podcasts" will reveal shows that meet your criteria.

Additionally, check out industry-specific websites, forums, and communities where your target audience is likely to congregate. These platforms often have dedicated sections or threads discussing relevant podcasts. Before asking for recommendations, engage with the community.

Social media is another excellent avenue to discover niche-specific podcasts. Consider joining industry-specific groups on platforms like Facebook, LinkedIn, and Reddit. Again, engage with the members before requesting show recommendations.

When looking for podcasts that fit your needs, your goal is to find out if the show will help you reach your target audience and increase brand awareness. Look for shows with a substantial and active listener base to maximize your exposure. Seek out information about the show's audience size, demographics, and engagement levels. Investigate how long the show has been running, who listens to it, and where they distribute interviews.

A useful metric for evaluating interview podcasts is the number of listens and downloads. These figures offer insight into the overall popularity and reach of the show. Although a show may have many downloads, if the listeners aren't actively engaged by listening in for at least a minute, it may not be the best match for your goals.

To gain a deeper understanding of a show's reach and engagement, look at listener demographics. Knowing the audience can help you determine if it aligns with your target audience, topics, and goals. Look for details such as age, gender, location, and listener interests.

Another factor to consider is the number of comments or reviews on podcast episodes, social media engagement (likes, shares, comments), and the frequency and quality of listener interactions with the host or their guests. High engagement levels suggest that the show has an active listener base willing to participate in discussions.

Take time to evaluate each show's production quality by reviewing past interviews. Your aim is to find and shortlist shows that offer high production value. They should have good audio quality, a clear interview structure, and engaging content. By assessing their production standards, it's more likely that your final interview will be of high quality.

Once you've confirmed that a podcast is a good fit and you've started a conversation with the host, inquire about the conditions for promoting your interview across your own distribution channels. If they don't allow you to promote your interview on your platforms, they may not be a good fit, and you should reconsider joining their show. However, if the host can demonstrate significant distribution channels and audience numbers, consider applying to be their guest.

Lastly, if you're new to podcast guest appearances, consider reaching out to hosts who are also starting their podcasting journey. They'll be eager to practice and may be open to your interview request. This way, both you and the host can learn and refine your skills. Your first few interviews may not be perfect, but to gain experience, consider pitching yourself to smaller shows.

Ownership and Permission

Even though you will play a significant role in the interview, it's important to inform the host about your plans before reformatting, redistributing, and promoting it on your own channels. While it's not always necessary, asking for permission shows that you value the host's input and reduces the potential for future disputes over its use.

Maintaining ownership and the rights to reuse, repurpose, and redistribute your interview content is essential for your podcast marketing strategy. Ensure you have control over how to use your content before recording each interview. For example, you may want to transcribe it into a blog post, create highlight reels for promotion, or share the entire interview. Always confirm with the host that you have the rights to use the content before agreeing to record.

While many hosts will encourage you to use your interview as you wish, it's important to communicate your intentions clearly. Discuss your plans for reusing the interview and obtain the necessary permissions to acquire a copy from the host, as well as to record a backup during the interview. Make sure the host understands your intended uses, such as video shorts, teasers, blog posts, or social media promotions. If needed, consider providing a release form or written agreement to formalize the approval process.

By acquiring permission and keeping copies of your interviews, you protect yourself against any disputes regarding the content and its use. The more transparent you are about your involvement in all aspects of the interview process, the easier it will be to demonstrate compliance with relevant privacy, copyright, and intellectual property requirements.

Booking Agents

Audiobooks are an incredible resource that have profoundly impacted my life in many ways. One audiobook that stood out was 'Buy Back Your Time' by Dan Martel. After listening to it, I realized just how much time I was spending on activities that I didn't enjoy. This prompted me to ask myself: if I didn't enjoy these tasks and they didn't bring out my best, then why was I doing them?

Naturally, I began to reevaluate how I spend my time and looked for ways to reclaim it without adding to my workload. Within a few months, after deciding to hire some help, I transitioned from being overloaded with unfulfilling work to focusing on things I enjoyed, which helped grow my business.

Regarding your interview-related tasks, if you're looking to reclaim your time, start by documenting all the activities associated with interviews that drain you. Make a list of everything you currently do related to interviews. This will only take a few minutes, but once you've outlined each task, you'll clearly identify which ones you want to delegate to someone else.

By applying this sorting process to your interview-related tasks, you may realize that searching for shows to appear on as a guest is also a draining activity. Personally, I found this task time consuming and exhausting. If you feel the same, consider delegating it to a dedicated interview booking agent. They can determine which podcasts suit you, conduct research to find a good fit, and handle all the pitching and record-keeping for you.

The best part of hiring a booking agent is that the work is taken off your plate, and they become responsible for finding interview opportunities. An added benefit is that booking agents often save time because of their existing relationships with hosts and their representatives.

When you engage a booking agent and outline your goals, they will search for new interview opportunities on your behalf. Once they identify potential appearances, they will pitch you to the hosts or their representatives. They create personalized pitches that highlight your expertise and show why you're an ideal fit for their show.

The real value in hiring a booking agent lies in not having to deal with communication, negotiations, or booking management yourself. The agent handles all these tasks for you. They are actively involved in discussing scheduling, interview format, duration, and addressing any specific requirements. They manage logistics, facilitate communication, and coordinate with both you and the host or producer to ensure a smooth booking process.

Once you find a great booking agent, focus on building a relationship with them. Your booking agent will work to understand your goals, preferences, and unique expertise to match you with relevant opportunities. By cultivating a trusted relationship, your agent will become a valuable source of information and your go-to resource for future interviews.

While having a podcast booking agent can be beneficial, not everyone chooses to use their services. Some prefer to do the legwork themselves, building relationships with hosts or leveraging personal connections for guest appearances. However, if you're busy or unfamiliar with the podcasting landscape, an interview booking agent can provide valuable expertise, industry connections, and ongoing support that saves you time and maximizes your interview opportunities.

Booking Interviews

If you're using an agent to manage your interview bookings, they will handle all aspects of your scheduling. Alternatively, if you're utilizing a dedicated podcast guest service for bookings, you'll have access to their online booking system. However, if you rely on a host's personal booking system, expect some variation in the process from one host to another.

Let's assume you've been accepted as a guest. At this point, you may have received an email outlining the booking process and possibly a link to a booking page where you can select a date and time for your interview. If so, great! Go ahead and schedule your call. Once that's done, depending on the booking system being used, you may receive an additional email with your booking details and a reminder SMS on the day of the call.

Thanks to technology, booking interviews has become much easier. It's increasingly common for hosts to use dedicated booking software or services to manage guest interviews. However, some hosts still do not use booking software. In fact, some hosts manually add dates and times to their calendars, often expecting you to do the same. This is a surefire way to make mistakes.

I know firsthand how embarrassing it can be to miss an interview. It's easy to forget a booking, not set a reminder, or get confused about the time zone differences when setting up the appointment. To help you avoid these errors and ensure you show up on time every time, we'll go through a typical interview booking process in this section to help you prepare better.

Once again, let's assume that you've secured an interview, the next step is to choose a date and time. As a guest on someone else's show, the host or their representative will usually provide a link to their booking page where you can select a suitable date and time. The host often, but not always, uses booking software to arrange the date and time for your interview. Popular options include Zoom, Calendly, Google Meet, and my current favorite, Book Like a Boss.

If the host uses booking software, you may receive a follow-up reminder email or SMS before your interview. If not, make it a standard practice to reach out to the host the day before to confirm that your interview is still on. This way, you'll know what to expect, and the host will appreciate that you're looking forward to the call.

Time zones can be a challenge for both hosts and guests. Depending on your location relative to the host's, it's easy to get confused about which time zone to use when booking the call. Fortunately, many hosts provide a link to their booking page, where guests can select their local time zone. The booking page will display a button showing your country, followed by your state, which automatically shows your local time zone. After you choose the location, date and time for your call, both you and the host will receive a booking email containing the call details in your respective time zones.

When booking interviews, ensure you allocate adequate time for preparation by scheduling your calls several weeks in advance. Keep in mind that the number of interviews you book each month depends on your available time and the timeline you've set to achieve your goals.

Regarding interview duration, if you plan to conduct longer, in-depth interviews lasting over an hour, you may only be able to commit to one or two interviews each month. Conversely, if you intend to do quick 10-15 minute interviews, you might manage to book four or five each week.

The number of interviews you conduct each month also depends on the goals you've established. For instance, if your organization seeks to promote various products and services to different market segments, you may need to allocate more time for interviews to accommodate that additional workload.

Remember, hosts dislike it when guests do not show up for their interviews. If you cannot make the call for any reason, which can occur occasionally, do the right thing by letting the host know and asking if it's possible to reschedule. The host will be much more receptive to rescheduling if you keep them informed. If there's no reason to miss the call, make sure that you're ready for your interview, and be there on time.

Tracking Outreach

If there's one podcaster I admire, it's Joe Rogan. On his show, The Joe Rogan Experience, he interviews talented and interesting people from various backgrounds. I appreciate that despite his extensive knowledge, Joe is genuinely curious about learning from his guests. Listening to hosts like him has taught me the importance of researching a host and their show before applying to be a guest.

Additionally, watching at least one of their interviews helps you understand their style and pace. If your potential host, like Joe, is naturally curious and more interested in your insights than in hearing their own voice, then that show should be on your outreach list.

As you reach out to multiple shows in the coming months and years, maintaining control over your outreach efforts will be vital. Create a simple database to track the hosts you've contacted and centralize their contact details and status. This database will help you prioritize your outreach and maximize your chances of getting booked, while also saving you time by avoiding duplicate efforts.

While there are several ways to create an interview spreadsheet, I recommend using Google Sheets for its simplicity. Include a host name column, a show name column, and a date column, along with three additional columns to track how many times you've contacted each host.

Once you've filled your outreach spreadsheet with a dozen potential shows, categorize and prioritize your outreach efforts. Create category columns to identify audience size, podcast popularity, and alignment with your goals. This information will help you focus on shows that align with your topics and promotional aims, allowing you to manage your time effectively and increase your chances of securing interviews on valuable podcasts. An outreach spreadsheet template is provided in the resources section of this book.

Pre-Interview Preparation

Preparing for your interview can boost your confidence and improve your performance. So, before each interview, invest some time to check out the host and their show. Listen to a few episodes, learn about the show's format and core audience, and get a feel for the host's style.

Create a list of key topics or points you want to address during your interview, and carefully and strategically prepare a narrative that resonates with your target audience. You should know your story in such detail that you can recite it line by line without hesitation. The stories you share must align with the problems and desires your target audience experiences and should be presented in a way that makes the listener think, "hey, that's just like me."

Although practice won't guarantee a perfect interview, it certainly helps. Rehearse your talking points out loud, either with a friend or by recording yourself. Doing this helps to refine your message and makes you more comfortable with the material. You can also use this practice time to pinpoint areas where you need to do more research or clarify your thoughts.

About an hour before your interview, check that your equipment is set up correctly. Run a test recording and check the levels using your preferred recording software. If you don't have any recording software, a free option is OBS Studio.

The environment where you record your interviews should be well-lit for video and organized to reduce unwanted noise. Noise can come from computer fans, pets, children, and other external sources that may be out of your control, unless you soundproof your recording space. Additionally, keep your phone in another room, as it always seems to ring during an interview.

When it's time for your interview, log into the interview room a few minutes early. This will allow you to talk with the host and check your audio and video settings before the call starts. Just before starting, let those around you know that you are about to give an interview and ask them to keep the noise down.

Key Messages

A key component of recording an effective interview is choosing relevant talking points. These points serve as a roadmap for your interview, guiding the conversation and ensuring you cover all important topics. They help you stay focused and organized, preventing rambling or going off topic.

To identify your key messages, ask yourself the following questions:

What is the main message or takeaway I want listeners to remember?

What features or benefits of my products or services should I highlight?

What pain points or challenges do my products or services address?

What sets my products or services apart from the competition?

Once you've answered these questions, narrow your key messages down to three to five main points. These will form the foundation of your talking points and help keep you focused during the interview.

Prior to the interview, identify your target audience's current beliefs for discussion during your interview, and compile them into the provided spreadsheet. In the first column, list all their current misconceptions related to your solution. In column two, add details about any experiences your prospects may have had that led to their current beliefs. Understanding the story they are telling themselves is crucial for addressing any wrong beliefs during your interview.

After identifying your key messages, structure your responses to ensure you share them clearly and effectively. A well-structured response makes it easier for listeners to follow and understand. When your interview is published, it will take some time to see which ones draw the most attention.

Using the Pareto Principle as a guide, once your content is live, monitor which interviews record the most interaction. Once you identify the content that resonates best with your audience, you can create more material that addresses their specific needs.

Mixing up your content also offers added benefits. Google values authentic, fresh content, and by regularly introducing new topics, your work is more likely to be noticed and ranked by Google's algorithm. While you can utilize your existing content for a long time, consistently creating and sharing new interview content will yield better results. Consistency is key to being noticed, so plan to frequently create fresh interview content. Choose a frequency that works for you and stick to it.

Local Recording

Although you are not responsible for recording the interview, it's wise to have a backup plan to prevent unexpected technical issues that could affect the final recording. For instance, if the host's recording fails to save properly, having a local copy on your computer can serve as a safety net. This way, both you and the host will have a reference file of the raw interview for future use.

One of the simplest and most cost-effective ways to create a local recording of your interviews is by using OBS Studio, a versatile and user-friendly software available for free. You can easily set it up by downloading OBS Studio from the link in the resources section. Before your scheduled interview, take some time to familiarize yourself with OBS Studio and ensure the program is configured to record and save your audio and video files.

Before recording the interview, run a test to confirm that the software is recording audio and video at appropriate levels and meets your expectations. Setting up OBS Studio at least a day before the interview gives you ample time for troubleshooting and helps ensure a smooth experience on the day.

If you choose not to record a copy of your interview, make sure you have the chance to review the recording before it goes live to catch any issues. Make it part of your interview conditions that you will receive an unedited copy. While you typically won't encounter anything unexpected, if you do find something you dislike or disagree with, you can ask the host to remove that section of the interview.

During The Interview

Your Role

As a guest, you're not responsible for producing the podcast or managing the technical aspects of recording and editing. Instead, you are invited to share your expertise and engage in a conversation with the host. Whether you are an entrepreneur, business owner, or expert in a specific field, being a guest offers a chance to showcase your knowledge and establish yourself as a thought leader and trusted authority in your industry.

Your role is to communicate your message clearly in a way that serves your target audience. Clear messaging helps prevent confusion and misunderstandings. Using jargon or unfamiliar technical terms can alienate your audience and cause them to lose interest. By simplifying your language and providing straightforward explanations, you can make your message accessible to a broader range of listeners.

Refining your core message is an ongoing process. As you gain experience and receive constructive feedback, continue to iterate and improve your responses. Reflect on past interviews and identify areas for adjustment that can enhance your messaging. Experiment with different approaches, storytelling techniques, and language to discover what resonates best with your audience.

Lastly, express genuine gratitude and appreciation to the host for having you as their guest. Thank them during the interview for the opportunity to share your insights. Afterward, send a follow-up email expressing your gratitude and reiterating how much you enjoyed the experience.

No Selling

Although I believe podcast interviews should be the centerpiece of your promotional efforts, they should not be used to push for quick sales. Listeners are savvy and will see through a product pitch disguised as an interview.

When someone tunes in to listen to your interview, they are looking to learn something valuable from you. They choose podcasts over nearly all other media because they appreciate the authenticity, expertise, and engaging conversations that this medium offers. They are not there to be sold to. When it comes to promoting your brand through podcast interviews, the key is to prioritize delivering value over making sales.

Confidence

If you're new to podcast interviews, it's common to feel a mix of excitement and nerves before a call. With practice and proper preparation, these feelings will diminish, allowing your confidence to grow. As you become more familiar with the interview process and gain some experience, you'll feel more at ease, and your authentic voice and expertise will shine through.

One way to boost confidence before an interview is to incorporate breathwork into your pre-interview routine. Inspired by experts like Gary Brecka, a prominent human biologist and wellness advocate, intentional breathing exercises can greatly impact your mental and physical state. Adding breathwork to your interview routine can enhance focus, reduce stress, and create a sense of calm. This simple process helps clear your mind, regulate emotions, and sets a positive tone for the conversation ahead.

In addition to breathwork, vocal exercises can enhance your confidence and performance during an interview. Vocal warm-ups, similar to physical warm-ups before exercise, are useful for optimizing your voice and articulation. Spend a few minutes before your recording session to read aloud or recite your interview notes to activate your vocal cords, improve diction, and enhance the clarity of your speech.

Be On Time

An important aspect of taking your guest role seriously is showing up on time every time. Punctuality and preparedness are signs of a true professional. If you want to make a good first impression, be online and ready for the host to let you into the interview room. If you're doing a studio interview, wait in the foyer for the host to greet you. Being timely not only leaves a positive impression on the host, but it also gives you a chance to settle in before the interview, allowing for a few minutes of conversation with the host beforehand.

Failing to arrive on time for a podcast interview can have several negative consequences. Firstly, it can disrupt the host's schedule and potentially delay the episode recording, affecting the host's availability and their planned content schedule. This disruption can lead to frustration and disappointment, impacting the relationship between you and the host. Additionally, arriving late can create a perception of unprofessionalism or a lack of respect for the host's time, which may influence the host's willingness to collaborate in the future or recommend you to other host's.

Moreover, being late can hinder your performance during the interview. Rushing in at the last minute leaves little time for mental preparation or adjustment to the environment, which can result in a less polished and engaging conversation. It can also increase anxiety, making it more difficult for you to connect with the host and convey ideas clearly. Conversely, being on time allows for a smoother transition into the interview, providing an opportunity to breathe, gather thoughts, and establish rapport with the host. This leads to a more relaxed and natural dialogue, enhancing the overall quality of your interview.

In addition to fostering a positive impression and ensuring a smooth interview process, being punctual also demonstrates commitment and reliability. It shows that you value the opportunity and respect the effort that goes into producing the podcast. This professionalism not only strengthens your relationship with the host but can also lead to additional opportunities in the future, as hosts are more likely to invite guests back or recommend them to their network when they are punctual and prepared.

Non-Attendance

Sometimes, unexpected situations can prevent you from attending a scheduled podcast interview. When this occurs, it's essential to inform the host as soon as possible. By communicating promptly with the host or their coordinator, they will understand your situation.

For instance, consider a guest who was set to share her insights as a successful surgeon. Eager to contribute, she was fully prepared for the interview. However, just hours before the recording, she faced an unforeseen situation that made her participation impossible.

Before the call, the guest sent a quick email explaining her unavailability. The host replied, and together they successfully rescheduled the interview.

This example highlights the importance of providing timely updates to hosts and their coordinators. A simple message can create a smoother experience and ensure that everyone is informed, making it easier to reschedule the interview.

Dress Code

Dressing appropriately for your interview is essential, especially for video calls. Your clothing choices can influence your confidence and how the audience perceives you. When you wear smart attire that makes you feel empowered and professional, it can positively impact your overall interview performance.

Whether you choose formal, business casual, or relaxed clothing, the important thing is to select outfits that reflect your personal style, boost your confidence, and align with your target audience. By focusing on these visual details and maintaining a cohesive look, you will record a professional looking interview that enhances your message and showcases your professionalism and expertise.

In addition to your outfit, when preparing for a video interview, think about your background. Choosing neutral or solid-colored clothing can help avoid distractions and make sure your attire works well with the surroundings. For example, be careful of colors that might blend into the background, like wearing green against a green screen, to avoid visual disruptions.

If you are not using a green screen, your choice of background can significantly enhance the overall visual presentation of your interview. A clutter-free, well-lit, and appealing backdrop can boost your professionalism. Some online meeting room platforms provide virtual backgrounds, allowing you to create a professional setting without needing physical props or green screens.

Interview Time

It's normal for an inexperienced guest to feel a little nervous. If you're feeling this way, let the host know and explain your feelings. In response, the host will do their best to ease your nerves by building rapport with you and guiding the conversation, much like two old friends chatting over coffee.

The host may ask some easy introductory questions that allow you to share who you are and what you do. If they're skilled, they'll inquire about something you genuinely enjoy or the people you love to spark a conversation that distracts you from the interview process altogether.

During your first few interviews, you may find yourself talking much faster than usual. Focus on speaking slowly and clearly, enunciating your words to ensure you are understood. Whenever possible, avoid filler words like "um," "like," and "you know."

To ensure you cover everything important during the call, keep track of the time. Be aware of your interview's start and finish times, and divide your list of questions into short time blocks. This will help you allocate a specific amount of time to answer each question.

Sometimes, when a host hears something interesting from you, they may want to ask off-script questions. If this occurs and you feel comfortable, feel free to discuss those topics. Keep in mind the time you have available. With practice, you will find it easier to keep your responses short and concise, allowing you to share your core message within the allotted time.

I remember interviewing a business owner whose body language suggested he was distracted and not fully engaged in the conversation. This was frustrating, as arranging the interview took time. He missed a valuable opportunity to share insights that could attract the right customers to his business. If you are going to give interviews, be present, take full advantage of the opportunity, and stay focused.

Video interviews reveal a lot about your body language, so maintain an upright posture throughout the call. Focus on the host, actively listen to their questions, and provide thoughtful responses. Avoid resting your elbows on the table, looking around the room, fidgeting, checking your phone, appearing bored, or crossing your arms.

During the introduction, the host will likely ask you to share something about yourself. This may or may not relate to the specific topic of the call and is often used to kick off the conversation. Not only does this give insight into who you are, but it also makes the interview more interesting and engaging.

Although you can share as much or as little about yourself as you wish, providing insights into your life and interests can influence the rest of the interview. Discussing where you live, your first entrepreneurial experience, influential people in your life, your educational and professional background, and your hobbies—such as your favorite music—can help set you apart from the typical business interview that often focuses solely on business matters and solutions.

Most experienced hosts know when to transition from the introductory conversation to the main part of the call. The core of the call is where the host concentrates on what you do and the problems your business solves. This is also when your business will be introduced, and you will talk about how you got involved in your current field.

The host may ask about your team, how you developed your business idea, who your ideal clients are, and even how you chose your business name. The topics mentioned are just examples, and you might prefer to be asked a completely different set of questions for each stage of your interview.

Although maintaining an upbeat and positive attitude is usually appropriate, if you need to share something that isn't very positive, do so, but return to the positive aspects of your story as quickly as possible. From my experience, it is better to close out an interview on a positive note. Sharing your story without becoming too negative can be challenging, but if you do it skillfully, it will highlight the best in you, your business, and the solutions you provide.

The final 5 minutes of your interview is the closing part of the call. This is your opportunity to provide your contact information or that of someone from your business. Depending on the topic, you might also use this time to introduce your onboarding process and share insights about the information available on your website. During this section, feel free to share your email address, social media details, phone number, website information, and any other relevant details.

To spark interest in your solution, share intriguing yet incomplete information during the call. This strategy encourages listeners to seek additional details that will complete the picture and provide answers. At the end of the call, invite them to visit your website for further information. The goal is to drive traffic to your landing page, encouraging listeners to either opt in for a special gift or book an initial consultation with you or your team.

Tell Compelling Stories

When we think about stories, it's clear how we've been conditioned to connect with them throughout our lives. I love when someone starts a conversation with "once upon a time" because I know what's coming. One of my all-time favorite stories is from Star Wars.

"A long time ago in a galaxy far, far away..."

I was young when Star Wars first hit the big screen, and I can remember that day as if it were yesterday. It began with my Nana taking me on an old silver bus into the city. We sat about halfway to the back of the bus with the windows open, listening to the sound of the diesel engine as we made our way to the movie theater. It was a magical experience, made even better by my Nana being at my side, and the movie impacted me so deeply that I will always remember it.

When we arrived, we bought our tickets and found our seats. Then that now-famous opening music started to play. Simultaneously, the big screen showed that iconic cascading yellow opening text as we began our journey through the stars. And then the sound of that opening scene, with the battle cruiser blasting onto the screen—wow, what an experience.

The entire storyline of Star Wars was a masterful example of storytelling. I didn't realize it at the time, but as each plot point and character was introduced, they became permanently etched in my mind. So much so that I ended up acquiring, or rather my Nana bought for me, every single Star Wars action figure there was to buy.

Beyond the magic of the movie theater, storytelling remains a crucial element in any setting, including podcast interviews. Stories help you engage with the audience and create a connection with them. And when delivered with care and authenticity, storytelling can increase the impact of your message, and make it more memorable and relatable.

One of the reasons why storytelling is so effective in an interview setting is that they help you connect with your audience on an emotional level. When you focus on sharing stories that speak to your listeners' dreams, desires, fears, and aspirations, and you share personal experiences, challenges, and triumphs, you establish a genuine connection on an emotional level that will move them one step closer to you and your business.

Your target audience needs to be at the center of everything you talk about during each interview. By focusing on their needs, interests and pain points, you can shape the stories you share in a way that not only touches them on an emotional level, you can also provide insights into ways they can solve their problems or achieve their goals, dreams and desires.

It's so important that you get good at telling your story above any technical knowledge you have about your products and services. For the right audience, the reason your stories are relatable is that they can help them feel as if you know what they're going through, which builds trust and familiarity with you and your business.

If you're still working on creating your own storytelling style, spend some time listening to how other guests give interviews. In this way, you will get an idea for how they speak, and you can model what you like, discard what you don't, and create your own unique storytelling style.

One of the key reasons interview storytelling is effective is that it helps to create a story arc. A 'story arc', or 'narrative arc' as originally created by Gustav Freytag, is the structure that shapes the flow of your story. This story arc consists of an introduction to the story, a series of events leading up to a climax, the climactic event, followed by a series of subsequent events, and finally, closing in some sort of resolution. When you use a story arc that has all of these elements, you can create a sense of anticipation and suspense that helps keep listeners engaged throughout your interview.

When you tell stories, your goal is to take listeners on a transformational journey. It's a journey from bad to good, poor to rich, sick to healthy, and so on. No matter what your solution offers, your storytelling must include a positive transformational outcome. Share stories that explain how you had a problem and then you found a solution to that problem. This is about the journey that led you to where you are today and includes what went wrong and what you did to fix it.

The thing here is who you or your client became as you told the story, and what you had to go through to become that person. What did it mean to become the person you are today because of it? The thing you need to work on is creating a story that not only helps people feel the emotion, but to show them how you went from a before state, where you were suffering or didn't have what you wanted, to the after state, where you were successful.

The next story you share is about the process you used to get your results. Listeners need to know everything you can share about the process you use so they know about it, and so they have a better understanding of how it helps them get the results they want.

Using the approach I'm sharing, you might already see your own narrative coming together. You're sharing your journey down a path from struggle to success, which is how effective stories have always been told. You're moving down the path on your own journey, which may be similar to things your target audience might also be experiencing. The only difference is, by listening to your story, your audience gets to fast track their own journey to success by learning from you instead of doing it the hard way like you did.

The ultimate outcome of your storytelling is to introduce a new way to solve a problem that your target audience already knows they have. You build a mental picture in their mind about their own situation which leads them to the solution, and from there, they can decide if what you're offering is right for them.

What relevant stories will you share during your interview that listeners will benefit from hearing? What will you tell them that encourages them to get more information from you, and what will you tell them to allay any fears they may have about your solution?

Lastly, when sharing your story, share the what, not the how. A listener's desire to know how to do something is the main reason they will seek out more information at the end of your interview. With that secret in mind, do not teach tactics or give direct answers to their problem during the call.

"People will do anything for those who encourage their dreams, justify their failures, allay their fears, confirm their suspicions and help them throw rocks at their enemies" - **Blair Warren**

Story Hooks

Although transformational story arc's are powerful, for them to grab your listeners' attention from the very beginning, you need to start telling your story with what is known as a hook. Your hook is a compelling, attention-grabbing statement or question that piques the listener's curiosity. This could be a thought-provoking question, an intriguing anecdote, or a surprising fact. By starting with a hook, you immediately draw the listener in and set the stage for an engaging and memorable interview.

By using descriptive language and imagery, you can transport your listeners to a specific time or place, making your interview more engaging and immersive. When describing a scene or setting, try to use sensory details that appeal to the five senses – sight, sound, smell, taste, and touch. This helps your audience to visualize the story and enhances their overall listening experience.

Creating suspense in your interview is another great way to keep your audience engaged and wanting more. Suspense can be created through the use of cliffhangers, unexpected twists, or unanswered questions. By strategically withholding information or building anticipation, you create a sense of suspense that keeps your listeners on the edge of their seats. This technique encourages your audience to stay tuned and listen until the end, making your interview even more impactful and memorable.

It's important to note that while storytelling is a powerful tool, it should be used strategically and authentically. The stories you share should be relevant to the topic at hand and provide value to your audience. Avoid using storytelling as a means of self-promotion or embellishing your experiences. Authenticity is key in creating a genuine connection with your listeners. So, be vulnerable, honest, and transparent when sharing your stories.

Make An Offer

Giving great interviews that lead nowhere is a pointless exercise. That's why, regardless of the solution your business offers, you should always make an offer near the end of each interview. To this end, many guests use free offers to attract leads and customers. Their free offer might include access to the basic version of their product or service to create awareness and interest. From there, they guide listeners toward their premium solutions.

Free offers are effective for attracting your target audience, particularly those who are hesitant to buy your core product or service. They spark conversations and allow you to showcase your solution while helping you build trust, credibility, and authority. This ultimately increases potential customers' confidence in you and your offerings.

Free offers also have viral potential. If your free offer is compelling, relevant, and valuable, satisfied users are more likely to recommend it to others. This can lead to organic growth and effective word-of-mouth marketing.

Use your free offers as a gateway to paid offers. This strategy often leads to increased conversions and a higher average lifetime value for your customers. For each free offer you provide, include one upsell offer of greater value. However, offering too many upsells can negatively affect how customers perceive your business. While your upsell sequence may boost your average sale value, limit yourself to a maximum of two additional offers.

Always include a free offer as part of your podcast marketing strategy. During the interview, share insights, tips, and tricks that listeners can use. Toward the end of the interview, discuss your special offer with the host and explain how listeners can access it. Finally, invite listeners to visit the landing page created just for them.

Your interviews and podcast marketing funnel represent the first phase of a multi-stage process, making your current leads the best prospects for additional sales opportunities. It's essential to create further marketing funnels that promote your premium back-end offers, as these can significantly impact conversions. By presenting additional offers, you not only boost revenue but also increase the lifetime value of each customer.

If your business offers multiple solutions, segment your audience into their respective funnels. This means you'll need a specific funnel for each solution your business provides. Since this process can take time, identify which solutions sell the most and prioritize recording interviews and creating related content for those products and services first, especially if resources are limited.

Call To Action

Renowned business consultant, marketing expert, and author Jay Abraham once said, "people are silently begging to be acknowledged, informed, given advance opportunities, and led into action." With this in mind, achieving the results you want from your podcast interviews requires you to give clear instructions for listeners who want to learn more about you, your business, and your offer.

A common mistake many guests make at the end of an interview is failing to present a clear call to action. Since this book focuses on using podcast interviews to promote your business, book, or venture, it's essential to prepare a specific call to action to share at the conclusion of each interview. The primary goal is to encourage listeners to visit your landing page, subscribe, and make a purchase.

While asking listeners to take action isn't difficult, it needs some planning to ensure you have an appropriate offer ready before each interview. As mentioned earlier, this preparation may include setting up a landing page where you can direct listeners to access your offer. For example, your call to action could be "download your free report by visiting mywebsite.com/offer" or "book your free consultation today at mywebsite.com/consultation."

As your interview nears its conclusion, the host will typically give you a chance to share your closing remarks. This moment is perfect for providing specific instructions for listeners to follow. You might outline steps for accessing an offer, a link to a landing page for a discount, or any action you want listeners to take next. Incorporate your call to action as a standard part of your interview process.

When you provide a clear, time-sensitive call to action, you promote effective communication between yourself and the listener. It's vital to ensure listeners understand what they need to do next and how to do it, increasing the likelihood that listener's will take the next step.

Encourage listeners to take the next step by offering discounts or special deals exclusively for them. This strategy creates a sense of urgency and exclusivity, motivating them to act quickly. For instance, you might provide a limited-time discount code or a bonus product for listeners who purchase or sign up within a specific timeframe. Be sure to emphasize that the offer is available only to interview listeners and will last for a short time.

When sharing your offer, consider using a strategy called "stacking the cool." This involves not just presenting your core offer but also enhancing it with bonus items, gifts, or additional downloads. The goal is to entice listeners to take advantage of your offer, making them feel like they're gaining something valuable by acting, while missing out if they don't.

Lastly, if you mention a specific closing date for your offer, ensure it reflects genuine scarcity. Your offer should truly expire and not be available after the designated period. Alternatively, if you plan to use your interview material long term, consider limiting the offer to a specific quantity.

"People are silently begging to be acknowledged, informed, given advance opportunities, and led into action." **- Jay Abraham**

Acknowledging The Host

Acknowledging the host is a critical component of closing an interview, as it fosters a sense of gratitude, professionalism, and mutual respect. Taking a moment to express your appreciation not only reflects well on you but also enhances the overall experience for both parties.

A thoughtful gesture, such as sending a thank-you gift or a handwritten note, can leave a lasting impact and significantly strengthen the relationship between you and the host. This act of kindness is not merely a formality; it is a sincere way to acknowledge the time, effort, and resources the host invested in producing the interview.

Acknowledging the host goes beyond a simple thank you; it demonstrates your commitment to establishing meaningful professional relationships. By recognizing the host's role in the interview's success, you signal integrity and respect for their contribution. This acknowledgment is particularly important as hosts juggle multiple responsibilities and appreciate being recognized for their hard work.

A personalized thank-you message, whether in the form of an email, a video, or even a social media shout-out, adds a human touch to the interaction and further strengthens the rapport between both parties. Such gestures show that you not only value the opportunity to share your insights but also recognize the collaborative effort that goes into creating engaging and informative content. This can enhance the overall experience for the host and make them more likely to remember you.

Building rapport and cultivating positive relationships with hosts can also lead to future opportunities and collaborations with other podcast hosts. When you leave a lasting impression through your acknowledgment, it showcases your professionalism and leaves a favorable impression that can open doors for future interviews, guest appearances, or even joint projects. Additionally, a strong relationship with one host can lead to referrals to others in their network, expanding your reach and influence within the podcasting community.

Thank You Email Example

Subject: Thank You for the Opportunity!

Dear [Host's Name],

I hope this message finds you well! I wanted to take a moment to extend my heartfelt thanks for having me as a guest on your podcast, [Podcast Name]. It was truly an honor to join you and share my insights on [specific topic discussed], and I appreciate the opportunity to connect with your audience.

The experience was incredibly enjoyable, and your thoughtful questions made for a dynamic conversation. I truly believe that we managed to engage listeners in a meaningful way, and I hope they found the discussion as valuable as I did.

Thank you once again for your hospitality and for providing such a wonderful platform for sharing ideas. I look forward to staying connected and hope to collaborate again in the future. If there's anything I can do to support you or your podcast, please don't hesitate to let me know!

Wishing you all the best and continued success with your show!

Regards,

Personal Performance

Regularly summarizing your personal performance after each interview is an invaluable practice that can significantly enhance your interview skills. By evaluating each interview, you can identify your strengths and pinpoint areas for improvement. For instance, if you frequently use filler words like "ums" and "ahs," it's essential to focus on enhancing the clarity and precision of your responses.

A strong start to your interview is vital for capturing listener interest and significantly reducing abandonment rates. Therefore, improving your interview performance begins with refining those opening minutes to create an interesting and compelling hook.

Obtaining and reviewing past interviews can provide valuable insights into your performance. Listening to these recordings allows you to assess your technique, delivery, and overall presentation skills, helping you enhance the impact and effectiveness of your content. Pay attention to your tone, pacing, and body language (if applicable), as these elements contribute to how your message is received.

Requesting feedback from the host is another effective way to gain new perspectives on your performance. Their insights may reveal valuable nuances you might have missed, such as your engagement level or how well you connected with the audience. Consider asking specific questions about your performance, such as whether your responses were clear and engaging or if there were moments that felt particularly strong or weak.

Another useful metric for evaluation is comparing the total recording time of your interview with the scheduled interview duration. If the interview ran longer than planned, it could indicate either the host's strong interest in your topic or suggest a need for a more concise conversation to ensure efficient content delivery. Strive for a balance between thoroughness and brevity, ensuring you provide valuable insights without overwhelming the audience.

After The Interview

Promotional Opportunities

After recording an amazing interview, the real work begins for the host or their editor. The editing process is meticulous and involves trimming pauses, removing "umms" and "ahhs," enhancing audio and video quality, and adding intro and outro music. Once editing is complete, your interview is ready for distribution. The host will then share it, optimizing it with tags and descriptions to maximize visibility and findability.

When your interview goes live, the host may create a blog post featuring the content, enriched with images and additional insights. They might also extract key takeaways and share quote graphics across various social media platforms to extend the interview's reach. Snippets can be turned into audiograms, and if the interview is in audio format, it may be converted into a video for distribution on YouTube, exposing it to a different audience.

Now that we've discussed what the host might do with your interview, what can you do with it? By following a similar distribution process across your own channels and choosing your own formats, you can increase the visibility and findability of your interview while extending its reach and impact.

As you work to grow your business, promote your book, or launch your latest project, it's essential to make the most of every promotional opportunity from your podcast interviews. Many podcast hosts offer promotional avenues for guests to boost their exposure. For instance, you might request a feature on the host's homepage, highlighting your interview episode for all their visitors. Some hosts provide onsite banner advertising, audio insert ads, and dedicated email promotions to their subscribers, all of which can significantly enhance your visibility.

To further enhance your promotional efforts, you could create engaging social media posts that spotlight key moments from the interview. Highlight compelling quotes, powerful sound bites, or behind-the-scenes photos that pique curiosity. Consider creating short video clips featuring highlights from your discussion and sharing them on platforms like Instagram, or LinkedIn, where dynamic content often engages users more effectively.

When sharing on social media, be sure to tag the host and mention the podcast's name to drive additional traffic to the episode. This tagging can often lead to the host sharing your post, reaching even more potential listeners.

Be sure to leverage your personal and professional networks. Share the interview with friends, family, and colleagues, encouraging them to listen, provide feedback, and share it within their networks. This grassroots approach can expand your reach as those closest to you help amplify your message.

Lastly, consider writing a blog post or newsletter summarizing the key insights from the interview. Link back to the interview and invite your audience to listen for more in-depth information.

Case Study - Promotional Opportunities

Sarah, a marketing consultant, recently appeared as a guest on a popular business podcast. Following the interview, she implemented a multifaceted promotional strategy. First, she reached out to the host, requesting feature spots on the podcast's homepage and sharing the interview with the host's email newsletter.

Sarah then shared the interview link across her social media platforms, tagging the host and using relevant hashtags to increase its visibility. She created engaging posts featuring memorable quotes from the interview, drawing attention and encouraging further interaction. For more dynamic content, Sarah produced a short video clip that captured key insights from the interview, which she shared on platforms like Instagram and LinkedIn.

Recognizing the importance of her blog, Sarah also wrote a post detailing the key takeaways from the interview, linking everything back to the podcast for her audience to access. Her proactive approach to promoting her presence on the podcast not only broadened her audience reach but also established her as a trusted authority, leading to increased inquiries about her services.

Through her strategic promotional actions, Sarah was able to leverage her podcast appearance as a significant driver of business growth, demonstrating the effectiveness of a well-rounded podcast marketing strategy.

Improvement Opportunities

Each interview presents unique growth opportunities, whether by delivering exceptional insights or highlighting areas that need improvement. Acknowledge successful interviews, but pay special attention to those that fell short. Use them as learning experiences to refine your guest appearances.

Consistent evaluation of your interview performances is key to identifying improvement opportunities. Analyze interviews that do not meet expectations to pinpoint areas needing attention. Experiment with new approaches in future interviews based on these insights.

If certain interviews fail to engage your audience effectively, consider scheduling new ones to address any shortcomings. Additionally, it may be helpful to remove or replace underperforming interview content that does not drive engagement or website traffic.

Feedback from listeners is also a valuable tool for identifying improvements, as it provides insights into audience sentiments and preferences. Actively addressing their feedback fosters relationship building and allows you to tailor content to better meet audience needs and expectations.

Adopting a meticulous approach to continuous improvement involves systematically documenting feedback, adjusting strategies, and tracking progress over time. Enter improvement opportunities in the spreadsheet provided and monitor the effectiveness of your podcast marketing strategy.

RSS Feed

I still remember the first time I encountered RSS feeds; they seemed puzzling and difficult to grasp. Fast forward to today, and I can't imagine efficiently distributing podcast content without them. RSS feeds, or Really Simple Syndication, are a web format used to publish content across various platforms, including blogs, news articles, email feeds, and podcasts. They enable you to share your latest content in a standardized, machine-readable format, making it easy for your audience to stay updated.

One key advantage of using RSS feeds to distribute your interview content is the timely updates they provide to end users. With an RSS feed, your subscribers receive notifications as soon as your latest interview goes live, ensuring they never miss an episode.

When you research where your target audience spends their time online, you'll find several platforms that support RSS feed integration. Popular platforms for distributing your podcast content via RSS include Apple Podcasts, Spotify, Stitcher, and YouTube Podcasts. You can even submit your RSS feed to over 50 different podcast directories and platforms, significantly expanding your reach. This means your interviews will automatically appear on various platforms, saving you time on manual uploads.

In addition to broadening your distribution, RSS feeds allow your audience to subscribe to your podcast content, enabling them to receive updates without checking manually. One of my favorite ways to receive updates is through my email client, where I can integrate RSS feeds for notifications directly in my inbox. This seamless integration keeps me informed while managing my other communications.

Using RSS feeds enhances your podcast marketing strategy. For instance, you can repurpose your interviews into blog posts or articles and then distribute those written pieces across your website and other platforms using your RSS feed. This not only helps reach a wider audience but also improves your SEO by creating backlinks to your original content.

When planning how to redistribute your interview content, consider the versatility of RSS feeds. They can automatically send your latest interviews to relevant platforms, increasing your content's reach and visibility without requiring any extra effort. This automation allows you to focus on creating more interview content while your existing interviews continue attracting new listeners across multiple channels.

Partnerships and Collaborations

As podcast interviews can lead to valuable partnerships and collaborations with hosts and business owners, express your interest in exploring these opportunities at the appropriate time. During these discussions, share specific ideas for potential collaborations. This demonstrates your enthusiasm and can attract the interest of hosts and business owners who may have connections that align with your business goals.

You can also enhance the exposure of your interview content by collaborating with other guest experts to cross-promote your interviews. Arrange guest swaps where both of you share each other's interviews across your networks. This strategy increases visibility, attracts new listeners, and fosters long-term, mutually beneficial relationships.

Leveraging your interviews for media features is another effective way to gain exposure and build credibility. Many journalists listen to podcasts to discover new and interesting stories, and being a guest on a popular podcast may catch their attention. After each interview, reach out to relevant journalists and media outlets to share the highlights of your latest conversation.

When contacting journalists, emphasize any unique insights you provided that could engage their audience. Tailor your message to fit their specific audience and show how your story aligns with their interests. Include a link to your interview along with relevant timestamps or quotes that showcase your expertise.

Social Media Redistribution

When redistributing your interview, it's essential to create engaging social media posts that highlight key takeaways and include clickable links directing listeners to your website for more information. This drives traffic to your site and enhances your interview's visibility.

Short-form videos are particularly effective for teasing your content and providing a sneak peek into the interview. From each interview, create a sixty-second video short and upload it to platforms like YouTube, Facebook and Instagram. These clips give your audience a taste of the discussion and can entice them to listen to the full episode. Consider using captions and engaging visuals to make these videos more appealing and accessible.

Highlight any positive feedback or testimonials you receive from listeners or industry experts as a result of your interviews. Sharing these endorsements on relevant social platforms can enhance your credibility and attract new listeners who resonate with the feedback.

When posting on social media, seize every opportunity to interact with your audience. Offer feedback, respond to inquiries, and provide additional resources to those who reach out after listening to your interview. This form of communication helps you build a loyal following and cultivate a network of brand advocates eager to promote your solutions.

If your schedule is packed and you find it challenging to share your latest interview, consider using automated distribution software to simplify the process. These tools can manage your content distribution with minimal input from you, allowing you to focus on creating new content. Options like SocialBee and Missinglettr can automate the sharing of your posts and even schedule the redistribution of previously shared content, ensuring that your interviews continue to reach new audiences over time.

Redistribution Sites and Timing

Although your interviews are an effective promotional tool, you shouldn't redistribute them on every available platform. It's important to be selective about where your interviews will reach your ideal audience for maximum exposure.

When an interview is ready for redistribution, consider the best time to share it across your network. This was a question I didn't think to ask when I started, which led to significant missed opportunities. I failed to recognize that most of my ideal audience was in a different time zone, meaning they were often asleep when I sent out my content.

To avoid wasting time, find the optimal times when your ideal audience is online and consuming content. With this information, you can determine the best times of day, according to their local time zone, when your audience is most likely to engage with your content. From there, you can schedule your posts accordingly.

As you research the best times to share your interview content, you may discover that your audience listens most during their morning commute, lunch break, or evening relaxation time. Understanding your audience and aligning your content distribution with peak listening times can help maximize your content's reach and impact.

Monday is one of the most popular days for listening to interviews. This trend can be linked to the start of the workweek, with many listeners using podcasts to ease into their day and get motivated for the week ahead. Listening during Monday morning commutes or while starting work tasks can provide a positive boost, especially when topics relate to personal growth, career development, or current events.

The most popular time for listening to interviews varies by audience. According to data from Edison Research, the morning commute is the busiest time, with 50% of weekly podcast listeners tuning in then. Other popular times include midday and evening, with 30% and 20% of listeners tuning in, respectively.

Weekends can also attract listeners, particularly Saturdays. Many people use weekends to catch up on their favorite shows, often binge-listening to multiple episodes. Some podcasts even release new episodes on weekends to align with their audience's habits.

The popularity of specific days and times for listening can also depend on the podcast's topic. For instance, a podcast about pop culture and celebrity interviews might be more popular during lunch breaks or evenings, while a podcast focused on personal finance may attract more listeners during their morning commute.

While morning interviews tend to reach a broader audience, distributing an interview in the evening might be more effective for those seeking personal growth or relaxation. Research indicates that audio-based interviews are generally more popular than video; however, this may be shifting. The convenience of listening on-the-go and the ability to multitask offer greater flexibility for listeners.

Additionally, interviews distributed later in the week often see lower audience engagement. If your goal is to engage with business owners, avoid redistributing interviews on Fridays, as many are winding down for the weekend.

Lead Nurturing

Nurturing leads who subscribe to your email list is essential for converting them into paying customers. This process increases your chances of conversion and fosters a loyal customer base. Effective lead nurturing involves providing valuable content while strategically incorporating marketing messages, significantly boosting engagement and trust over time.

Since you already understand your subscribers' needs and preferences, you can segment them based on their behavior and interactions with your content. This enables you to tailor future email communications to resonate with each individual, enhancing the relevance of your messages.

To save time, utilize email automation to streamline your nurturing efforts. Automation allows you to send timely, personalized content that aligns with your leads' interests. For example, you can offer educational resources, exclusive deals, and helpful tips tailored to their specific requirements. This targeted approach keeps your audience engaged and positions you as a valuable resource in their decision-making process.

Throughout the nurturing journey, focus on building trust and rapport with your subscribers. Share success stories, testimonials, and case studies that highlight the benefits of your products or services. This not only reinforces your credibility but also helps potential customers envision the positive impact of your offerings on their lives.

Lead nurturing is a gradual process. Don't be discouraged if a subscriber doesn't make an immediate purchase; nurturing requires patience and persistence. By consistently delivering valuable content and personalized marketing messages, you create a nurturing environment that encourages leads to progress through your sales funnel.

Repurposing Interview Content

As anyone who collaborates with me knows, I am a strong advocate for repurposing podcast interview content. This strategy not only broadens your reach and enhances visibility but also maximizes the value you provide to your audience, allowing you to extract greater mileage from your original content. By diversifying the formats in which you present your material, you can attract new audiences who may not have discovered you through a single channel.

Repurposing your interview content is a powerful way to amplify your promotional efforts while gaining valuable insights into your ideal audience. When you adapt your content thoughtfully, you engage listeners in new ways and increase awareness of your business and its solutions.

To effectively repurpose your content, start by considering the formats that will resonate most with your target audience. For instance, if you have recorded an audio interview, you can transform it into engaging video content. This could include creating both long-form and short-form videos, utilizing features from various editing tools to add dynamic elements like animated graphics, backgrounds, and text captions. Once edited, you can share these videos as YouTube Shorts or Instagram or Facebook Reels—ensuring you select the platform that aligns best with your audience.

Moreover, you can also convert your interviews into downloadable transcripts, eBooks, and guides. This not only provides your audience with a wealth of valuable resources but also positions you as an authority in your field. These materials can serve as lead magnets, enticing potential clients to subscribe to your content or engage further with your offerings.

Short Form Video

Having followed author and business coach James Schramko for many years, I've noticed his willingness to adapt and innovate in response to changing trends. For example, he transitioned from operating under the name Superfast Business to using his own name for branding after research indicated greater engagement potential. This shift demonstrates his commitment to evolving his brand to better connect with his audience.

In line with this adaptability, James has embraced short-form video as a powerful way to repurpose various types of content, including podcast interviews. I vividly remember the first time I encountered a short-form video on Facebook, and it was one of James's creations.

Short-form videos typically last between one and three minutes, compelling creators to distill their most relevant information into a concise format. With the abundance of editing software available today, transforming segments of long-form interviews into engaging short-form videos has never been easier. These videos are gaining traction across multiple platforms, including Facebook, Instagram, YouTube and Snapchat, although they may go by different names on each.

As Gary Vaynerchuk wisely states, "Attention is the name of the game," and short-form videos excel at capturing that attention. Formats like YouTube Shorts and Instagram Reels not only convert your content into digestible clips but are also easy to produce. Because these videos require significantly less time for viewers to watch, they're also very appealing.

To illustrate the effectiveness of short-form videos, consider that YouTube launched its Shorts feature in September 2020, with these videos now attracting over 3.5 billion daily views, 70% of which come from mobile devices. Given their growing popularity, converting long-form interviews into a series of short-form videos can maximize promotional impact. For instance, a thirty-minute interview could yield at least a dozen short-form videos that spotlight key moments and insights.

Short-form videos can effectively tease your full interview by sharing snippets of engaging conversations or highlighting essential topics discussed. For example, a brief clip of you sharing a compelling fact or personal story can spark curiosity and encourage viewers to seek out the full interview.

Moreover, short-form videos can serve as a comprehensive overview of the interview by combining clips, visuals, and text overlays that emphasize key takeaways. This multimedia approach creates a visually engaging and informative summary, making it more shareable and likely to reach a wider audience.

If you're a book author, consider using short-form videos to focus on specific aspects of your writing journey. For instance, you could create separate videos discussing your mission, writing tips, or challenges faced during the writing process. By tailoring these clips to different segments of your market, you can engage various audiences interested in specific subtopics related to your book.

To drive viewers back to your full interview, always include a clear call-to-action at the end of your short-form videos. Whether you want them to subscribe to your channel, follow you on social media, or listen to the complete interview, ensure you guide them on what to do next.

Additionally, it's crucial to include your website address in the video. This way, if viewers are intrigued and want to learn more, they can easily visit your site. While short-form video is a powerful tool, remember that any video format can be leveraged to direct your audience back to your website and your offerings. By creatively utilizing short-form videos, you can significantly enhance your promotional efforts and engage a broader audience with your podcast interviews.

Images

Incorporating high-quality images into your redistribution strategy is crucial, especially when promoting your podcast guest interview. With advancements in technology, including AI generated images and graphic design tools, creating captivating visuals that tell a story has become easy and efficient.

Using images strategically across various social networks can enhance your promotional efforts significantly. For instance, you can design eye-catching JPEGs or GIFs to share on platforms like Instagram, Facebook, X, and LinkedIn. Each platform has preferred image dimensions and formats, so it's essential to tailor your visuals accordingly.

For Instagram, consider using carousel posts to share multiple images, such as quotes from the interview, behind-the-scenes shots, or highlights of key discussion points. This format encourages users to swipe through your content, boosting engagement. On X, a single impactful image can quickly capture attention and encourage reposts, while on LinkedIn, a professional-looking image can enhance your credibility and resonate with a business-focused audience.

High-quality images serve as powerful tools for conveying your personality, opinions, and interests. They help establish a connection with potential listeners even before they engage with your content. For example, you can create graphics that visually summarize the main topics discussed in your interview, making it easier for your audience to grasp your insights at a glance.

AI tools can assist in generating visuals that reflect your discussion themes, whether it's an infographic illustrating key statistics or a stylized quote graphic that resonates with your audience. For instance, if your interview covers the importance of mental health, you could create an infographic that highlights key statistics about mental health awareness, which can be shared on platforms like Pinterest or Instagram.

If you prefer a more personal touch, consider taking a screenshot of yourself and the host during the interview. These candid images can be shared alongside a summary of key points, making the content more relatable and easier to digest. Such visuals not only break up text-heavy posts but also add a human element that can attract more engagement. For example, sharing a fun, candid moment from the interview can humanize the experience and encourage your audience to connect on a personal level.

Additionally, animated GIFs featuring highlights from the interview can be particularly effective on platforms like Instagram Stories. These formats are designed to capture attention quickly and encourage viewers to seek out the full interview. For instance, you might create a 15-second clip featuring a compelling quote or an intriguing question posed during the interview. This can entice viewers to click through to listen to the entire episode.

When creating your promotional images, utilize tools like Canva, which offer customizable templates. This helps you maintain a consistent brand aesthetic across all your visuals. Not only does this enhance your professionalism, but it also makes your posts instantly recognizable to your audience.

Incorporating user-generated content can also amplify your reach. Encourage your listeners to share their own images or thoughts related to the interview and tag you in their posts. This not only fosters community engagement but also provides you with additional content to share on your channels.

Books

Another effective way to repurpose your interview content is to compile a book from your previous interviews. While this may seem daunting at first, creating a valuable book from your podcast content can be incredibly rewarding. As you conduct more interviews, you'll gather a wealth of material that can be transformed into a book with the help of transcription technology.

Many niche interview guests have successfully turned their podcast appearances into published works. For instance, business coaches often compile insights from various entrepreneurs they've interviewed, resulting in a book that features different perspectives on success and strategies for growth.

Similarly, health and wellness experts might gather interviews with nutritionists, fitness trainers, and mental health professionals to produce a comprehensive guide to holistic health. Authors like Tim Ferriss have also leveraged their podcast interviews to create bestselling books, such as "Tools of Titans," which distills lessons from numerous guests into actionable insights.

Writing a book based on your interview content is a fantastic way to repurpose material that might otherwise be overlooked. Having your own published book not only enhances your credibility but also allows you to make a more significant impact and reach a broader audience across various platforms. Additionally, you can cater to diverse preferences by offering both written and audio versions of your book, appealing to those who enjoy audiobooks.

Compiling a book from your interviews also enhances your personal brand, providing recognition for the effort you've put into creating the book. This format allows you to delve deeper into each conversation, adding stories and insights that complement the original content and offer greater value to your readers.

However, there are some considerations to keep in mind when using your interview content to write a book. One important factor is the time needed to gather enough interview material to create a cohesive and useful book. For example, if you plan to use a thirty-minute interview as a basis, ensure that the topics discussed are comprehensive enough to contribute to your book's overall narrative.

To effectively plan your book, start by researching topics relevant to your expertise, business, and audience. From there, schedule interviews focused on those themes. For example, if you're a marketing expert, consider being interviewed about your marketing strategies, challenges, and successes. This will provide you with a rich pool of content that can be woven together into a cohesive narrative.

Transcriptions

Another effective way to maximize the value of your interview content is by creating transcripts. Transcripts enhance the accessibility and searchability of your interviews and serve as valuable lead magnets that guide potential customers to your products and services. By providing a written version of your audio content, you cater to diverse audience preferences, making it easier for those who prefer reading to engage with your material.

Creating transcripts is straightforward and can significantly boost your content strategy. They can be easily stored and repurposed into various formats, including blog posts, social media snippets, and used in other promotional campaigns. For instance, you can extract compelling quotes or key insights from the transcript to create visually appealing graphics for platforms like Instagram or X, further amplifying your reach.

While there are several noteworthy transcription services available, I personally use two: Happy Scribe and Castmagic. Both platforms efficiently convert your interview audio into accurate text in just a matter of minutes. Once transcribed, you can upload the text to your website, blog, or social media, enhancing the accessibility of your content. Including timestamps, key discussion points, and notable quotes in your transcripts makes the details of your interview more digestible for various audiences, especially those who prefer reading over listening.

Castmagic stands out as an AI-driven platform with a range of powerful features. Beyond simply generating an accurate transcript, it produces engaging headlines, relevant keywords, and suggested titles based on specific prompts you provide. For example, after uploading your longform interview content, you can receive a list of catchy headline options for your blog posts or social media promotions. Additionally, it generates a complete list of social media content formats, saving you hours of time in redistribution efforts.

Your interview transcripts can serve as lead magnets by offering them in exchange for email subscriptions. For instance, you could create a downloadable PDF version of the transcript that highlights the key insights from the interview. This not only encourages engagement but also helps you build your email list, allowing you to nurture relationships with your audience over time.

Transcripts can also enhance your SEO efforts. By including the transcript on your website, you create additional text for search engines to index, which can improve your visibility in search results. This is particularly beneficial for long-tail keywords related to the topics discussed in your interviews. For example, if your podcast guest discusses effective marketing strategies, having a transcript that includes those keywords can help attract more organic traffic to your site.

Testimonials and Referrals

Although podcast interviews effectively promote your business, book, or project, it is essential to utilize testimonials and referrals to maintain visibility with your target audience after the interview ends. This approach builds your credibility, expands your network, and creates new opportunities that might not have been available otherwise.

World-renowned marketing expert Jay Abraham emphasizes the significance of testimonials and referrals in his book "The Sticking Point Solution," describing them as powerful marketing tools essential for building credibility and attracting new customers. Moreover, a study by McKinsey found that 20% to 50% of purchasing decisions are influenced by word-of-mouth.

A notable example of word-of-mouth marketing comes from Phil Knight, the founder of Nike. When local stores initially rejected his products, Phil began selling shoes from the back of his car at track meets. By connecting with runners and coaches, he eventually received orders as enthusiasm for his products spread.

While testimonials and word-of-mouth marketing significantly influence consumer behavior and help establish trust in your business and solutions, word-of-mouth is more organic and personal, whereas testimonials are more formal and will feature in your promotional efforts.

The true strength of word-of-mouth marketing lies in how a brief, positive conversation about you, your business, and the solutions you provide can affect someone's buying decision. This influence occurs because the opinion comes from someone they trust.

To harness the power of word-of-mouth, focus on delivering exceptional interviews along with high-quality products and services that deliver results. An ideal scenario occurs when someone listens to your interview, becomes a satisfied customer, and then shares their positive experience with friends and colleagues. When people discuss your interviews and the solutions your business provides without any prompting from you, generating sales becomes much easier.

Host Testimonials and Referrals

To make your guest interview strategy effective, you need a reliable method for finding and booking new interviews. A simpler way to speed up your next interview is to use host testimonials and referrals. This approach leverages the current host's credibility to open up new interview opportunities.

Including testimonials in your podcast pitch kit or guest profile is essential for your interview campaign's success. Use these testimonials when reaching out to new hosts. By gathering testimonials, you create a portfolio of evidence that enhances your promotional toolkit. From your very first interview, make it a habit to ask each host for a testimonial and a referral in your preferred format.

When a host refers you to someone else, it signals that you are knowledgeable and trustworthy. A host referral can significantly expand your interview opportunities by introducing you to new hosts and an audience that values their judgment and expertise. This wider exposure not only leads to more interviews but also boosts your visibility and credibility, ultimately resulting in new leads and increased conversions.

Host referrals are effective because they reduce the time spent researching and contacting new hosts. Since referrals are personal endorsements, they make it easier to expand your interview network, simplifying the process of securing interviews compared to cold contacting hosts. When one host refers you to another, their endorsement emphasizes your competence and the quality of your content, suggesting that you would be a valuable addition to their lineup.

Picture yourself as a podcast guest specializing in digital marketing strategies for small businesses. Through engaging and informative appearances, you share valuable insights with both the host and their audience. In turn, you always ask the host for a testimonial and a referral. You then use these endorsements to showcase your experiences and demonstrate your expertise to future hosts.

Timing Your Request

As timing is crucial, be sure to ask for a testimonial and a referral to other hosts immediately after your interview concludes. Start this conversation by acknowledging the time and effort the host dedicated to the interview. Thank them for their participation and invite any feedback that could help you improve your performance. Clearly express your eagerness to share your message with other hosts who would benefit from your content.

Since hosts are often busy, make it easier for them to provide testimonials and referrals by giving them a link to a dedicated page on your website. When you receive their feedback, send a thank-you email to acknowledge it. When sending your testimonial and referral link, simplify the process for the host with a few straightforward questions. For example, you might ask: What did I discuss during the interview that you found particularly relevant to your audience? What topics do you wish I had covered more? And what kind of content can I share that would better serve your audience in the future?

If the current host can't recall another host they would recommend right away, offer to send a follow-up email in a couple of days. This way, you relieve the pressure of thinking of a referral on the spot. If the host does provide potential contacts, add them to your interview spreadsheet and follow up.

Outsource The Work

If you're the only person in your business and don't have time to redistribute your interview content, consider outsourcing. Although you will need to spend time training external workers, once they are familiar with the process, you'll save time and gain the freedom to focus on other aspects of growing your business.

Additionally, to further lighten your workload, consider using dedicated distribution software to streamline interview redistribution. As some platforms do not integrate with automated distribution tools, you may still need to hire external help for managing redistribution on those sites.

If your budget allows, you might choose to hire an agency to create a complete promotional strategy and handle all your redistribution needs. Personally, I prefer hiring a virtual assistant, as they can manage most of my interview-related tasks, including redistribution and promotion across various channels in a range of formats. When hiring, look for someone with promotional experience in your niche and a proven track record of similar work. Before hiring, share your goals and expectations, and evaluate their experience and current rates.

When hiring, be clear with candidates about your promotional goals. Are you aiming to build an email list, drive traffic to your website, or generate more sales? Whatever your objectives are, having specific goals will aid in finding the right person for the job. To facilitate the hiring process for similar roles in the future, provide a detailed role description outlining the scope of the role, required skills, and key responsibilities.

Although there will be an initial training phase, once your assistant is up to speed, they will help you manage many, if not all, of your interview-related tasks. These responsibilities can include creating and scheduling social media posts, monitoring engagement, and responding to comments and messages.

After hiring, maintain regular communication about your expectations, goals, and the progress they've made. This will ensure alignment with your overall promotional strategy. Be open to their suggestions and address any issues promptly to help them consistently deliver their best work.

Measuring Performance

Growing up, I remember the delightful scent of my nana's beloved apple pie wafting through the house, a comforting aroma that always drew attention. While she perfected her recipe over the years, she sometimes introduced new ingredients or techniques to enhance the pie's flavor. By diligently noting each change's impact on taste and texture, she refined the recipe through careful measurement and ongoing adjustments. Analyzing the results, she fine-tuned cooking times and ingredients, ultimately creating an incredible apple pie.

In podcast marketing, the process of testing, measuring, and improving mirrors the precision of baking nana's apple pie. Just as she experimented with ingredients, you can try various methods to enhance your interviews, evaluating which strategies resonate most with the audience. Additionally, by testing different distribution channels, you can identify the platforms that generate the highest listener engagement and assess the impact of each interview on your website traffic.

Through rigorous testing and measurement across all aspects of your podcast marketing strategy, you will discover the optimal approach. With these insights, you can refine your strategies to boost the effectiveness of your guest appearances, attract a larger audience, nurture leads, and drive conversions with greater consistency.

"Testing is nothing more than methodically putting to a vote, one supposition against another"

- Jay Abraham

Performance Tracking

To evaluate the effectiveness of your podcast marketing efforts, tracking and analyzing audience insights and performance metrics is essential. By comparing data from various interviews and sources, you can uncover trends, identify areas for improvement, and assess the impacts on key metrics such as website traffic and conversion rates.

The Pareto Principle, commonly known as the 80/20 rule, suggests that 80% of your results come from just 20% of your efforts. In podcast marketing, this means that a small number of interviews can significantly boost overall engagement and outcomes. Therefore, identifying the crucial 20% of interviews that generate 80% of listener interaction is key to refining your promotional strategies and understanding which themes resonate most with your audience.

If you don't receive performance data from podcast hosts, consider capturing and redistributing your interviews to track their reach. Many podcast hosting platforms offer valuable analytics on listens and audience engagement, giving you insights into which interviews drive traffic to your landing pages.

While attracting traffic to your site is vital, the ultimate goal is to convert that traffic into leads and sales. The conversion rate is a key performance metric that measures the percentage of website visitors who complete specific actions, such as subscribing to a newsletter or making a purchase. To calculate conversion rate, divide the number of conversions by the total number of visitors. A conversion rate of 2% or higher from interview referrals indicates that those interviews effectively engage the right audience.

Email marketing is another cornerstone of a successful podcast marketing strategy, providing a direct channel to nurture relationships with listeners and promote episodes. To measure the effectiveness of your email campaigns, focus on metrics such as open rates, click-through rates, conversion rates, and subscriber growth. These insights not only reveal how well your content resonates with your audience, the data helps you tailor future campaigns and ensure your messaging remains relevant and engaging.

Finally, social media platforms are crucial for engaging your audience and amplifying your podcast interviews. Monitor engagement metrics like shares, likes, comments, and click-through rates. Likes and shares indicate how well your content resonates with listeners, while comments provide valuable feedback. After posting your interview on social media, use tools like Facebook Insights and X Analytics to review performance. Monitoring these metrics will help you determine which content drives the most engagement, allowing you to refine your marketing efforts and strengthen the relationship with your audience.

Interview Library

When embarking on your podcast marketing journey, it's essential to prioritize backups of your interviews. Many guests initially overlook the need for this precaution, assuming that the host will take care of recording and production. However, this assumption can lead to unexpected consequences, as demonstrated by our guest, Emily.

During her interview, Emily was excited to share her insights on personal development, only to learn that the host had encountered technical issues and lost the recording. This experience taught her a crucial lesson about recording her interviews locally, giving her peace of mind and readily available backups in case something goes wrong in the future.

Hosts also face the uncomfortable reality of losing high-quality interviews with exceptional guests. After engaging in insightful conversations with industry leaders, a host may be devastated to discover that their interview had audio issues that rendered it unusable. The embarrassment of informing a guest about recording mishaps and requesting a re-recording can be a significant setback, underscoring the importance of maintaining control over your interview recordings.

Common reasons for lost recordings often stem from hardware or software failures. Technical issues, such as hard drive crashes or computer malfunctions, can lead to permanently corrupted files that are unrecoverable. Even files that are saved successfully can become corrupted and unreadable. Additionally, external factors beyond anyone's control—such as theft or fire—can result in the loss of interview files.

Recognizing these potential risks emphasizes the need for a simple system for creating and storing backups. By establishing a backup routine, you can significantly reduce the likelihood of losing valuable content.

Adopting a systematic approach to managing your interview data not only minimizes the risks of loss but also facilitates the retrieval and repurposing of material across various formats and platforms. For example, long-form podcast interviews can be distilled into shorter video segments, allowing for broader engagement and distribution opportunities.

Furthermore, an organized interview library serves as an essential research resource. As it grows, you can identify trends and track changes over time, ensuring that you stay informed about the latest developments in your industry. If you need to reference a past statement, having an organized interview archive allows for swift access to supporting evidence. Including time stamped transcripts alongside each interview also enables quick referencing of key points without replaying the entire episode.

Access to recorded interviews is particularly beneficial for showcasing your expertise and accomplishments. Having a personal portfolio of interviews enhances your credibility and provides real-life examples of your knowledge. Sharing these recordings during pitches to potential clients, at speaking engagements, or through collaborative opportunities further strengthens your status in your chosen field.

Library Maintenance

Maintaining an organized and up-to-date library of your previous podcast guest interviews is essential for several reasons. Regularly reviewing your interview recordings, edited files, and related materials ensures that your library remains relevant and easily accessible.

One key benefit of having a well-organized interview library is the ease with which you can reference past content when creating new episodes or promotional materials. By keeping meticulous records of your interviews, you can quickly extract insights, memorable quotes, or recurring themes that align with current trends or audience interests. This approach enhances your content strategy and enables you to produce more cohesive and impactful material. For example, if you've appeared on multiple podcasts discussing entrepreneurship, you can compile those insights into a special episode or a blog post, showcasing diverse perspectives that add additional value for your listeners.

Regularly updating your library also allows you to identify content that may be outdated or no longer aligned with your brand's messaging. While keeping valuable content is important, removing or archiving interviews that no longer reflect your current focus helps safeguard your credibility. If you're concerned about needing that content in the future, consider saving it in a separate folder or archive instead of deleting it entirely. This way, you preserve the potential to revisit and repurpose it when necessary while keeping your active library streamlined and current.

Case Study - Library Maintenance

Let's imagine that Jason, an aspiring entrepreneur and podcast guest, has just completed a successful interview on a popular business podcast. Delighted with the experience, he knows that having a copy of the recording is just the beginning. As time goes on, that single interview file could multiply into several copies, potentially leading to confusion if he doesn't have a proper system to manage his files. Without such a system, misplacing or mislabeling interviews becomes easy, making it challenging to find specific recordings when needed.

With this in mind, Jason takes the first step in creating a solid backup, storage, and retrieval system. He sets up a designated folder on his computer specifically for his podcast interviews. Within that folder, he creates subfolders for each podcast appearance. To complement this, Jason builds a comprehensive spreadsheet to track essential details about each interview, including the host's name, podcast show name, interview title, release date, a brief description, and key timestamps that highlight relevant discussion points.

Recognizing the importance of backups, Jason saves at least two copies of the file and any related documents. One copy resides on his local hard drive while another is uploaded to Google Drive for additional security.

Jason further improves his file management by adding columns in his spreadsheet to categorize interviews by topic. For instance, if he has multiple interviews centered around "Startup Growth Strategies," he cross-references those entries, making it easy for him to locate similar discussions when preparing for future engagements or promotional efforts. By establishing this organized system early on, Jason ensures that his podcast interview library remains manageable, accessible, and efficient for ongoing use, helping him streamline his podcast marketing efforts.

3-Part Interview Checklist

To assist you in developing your own unique podcast marketing system, I've created a 3-part interview checklist to guide the entire interview process and conversation flow between you and the host.

By dividing the interview checklist into three distinct phases—before the call, during the call, and after the call—you create a clear framework for effective coordination at each stage. Mapping out the interview process visually helps connect each phase with specific conversation points, additional information, and follow-up actions.

The main benefit of using the checklist is ensuring thorough preparation, which reduces last-minute stress and enhances your confidence before the interview. With this well-crafted checklist, you can plan and execute each step without overlooking important discussion points.

This checklist also helps prevent technical mishaps and ensures a seamless interview experience. Tasks such as checking audio and video settings, testing the microphone, verifying internet connectivity, and optimizing the recording environment are all included. Regularly confirming these technical aspects before each call minimizes the risk of interruptions, improves audio and video quality, and elevates your overall professionalism during the interview.

To maximize the impact of each interview, use the checklist before the call to collaborate with the host on key details. Regularly consult the checklist before, during, and after each call to ensure accountability and that all necessary steps are taken for a successful interview performance.

Congratulations!

You've reached the end of 'The Greatest Podcast Marketing Book Ever Written.'

Having worked through this book, you now understand that podcast interviews are a powerful promotional tool for your business. They offer a unique way to build awareness, educate listeners, and promote your business, book or venture.

You have also learnt that podcast marketing is more than just giving interviews. It is a coordinated effort that involves communication, preparation, commitment, systems, and dedication and persistence to consistently create impactful and engaging content that delivers results for your business.

By appearing on relevant podcasts, you will reach a broad audience and establish yourself as an expert in your field. This opportunity allows you to share your story, build credibility and trust, and generate leads and sales for your business at a fraction of the cost of traditional marketing.

Long after you finish reading this book, you will reach the impressive milestone of 100 interviews. As you work towards this goal, you will become a master storyteller, sharing every relevant aspect of your journey. You'll inspire your audience and become someone they know, like, and trust.

Soon, your interviews will be available for everyone to listen to. Many listeners, most of whom you will never meet, will leave comments praising you and acknowledging how something you said during an interview made a significant impact.

If you wish you had started earlier, I completely understand. I know it can feel too late since you're looking for results now. But I'm here to tell you that it's not too late, and the best time to start is today!

If you're feeling overwhelmed by everything you need to do, remember that you don't have to tackle everything at once. The most important step is to start. Don't wait any longer—plant your seed and watch it grow as you take it one step at a time, day by day.

As we approach the end of the book, I have a few final suggestions. If you're already marketing your products and services through other methods, keep it up. This will support you as you build your podcast marketing system and gain momentum.

As you get more familiar with podcast marketing, assess how much time you can dedicate to it and commit that time to developing your new strategy. Set aside some weekend hours or focus on it before or after your workday, depending on your current commitments and preferences. Whatever you decide, stick to it and prioritize it.

If you start and then hit a plateau, don't be too hard on yourself. It's part of the process, and everyone faces moments when it feels like they're hitting a brick wall. For example, you might record a fantastic interview and share it, only to notice a lack of views or engagement afterward. As I mentioned earlier, content marketing takes time—lots of time. Even after recording and sharing great interviews for six months, you're still in the early stages. Given how long it can be to gain momentum, it's important to keep moving forward, keep recording, and keep sharing new interviews. Just don't quit!

Somewhere along the way, one of your interviews will gain enough attention that the early struggles will fade away. A good rule of thumb is that out of ten interviews, eight will perform well, while two will truly excel. So, continue recording interviews, share your content consistently, pay attention to your audience's responses, and adjust accordingly.

No matter what you do or how hard you try, you will never create a perfect sales pitch, interview, or landing page. This does not matter. All you need to do is get started, keep going, and ensure that all the elements of your podcast marketing system are in place to achieve results. I know this system works.

The most important point I want to make is this: if you don't create and share your content, no one will discover it or ever be in a position to buy your solutions. It's crucial to set a solid foundation now and refine it later. That initial momentum leads to exposure and then to results, and those results will encourage you to keep moving forward.

"The best time to plant a tree was twenty years ago, the second best time is now" **- Chinese Proverb**

Resources

Below you will find a link to your **PODCAST MARKETING PACK.**

Click the link below and make a copy of the spreadsheet.

https://links.myfuturebusiness.com/spreadsheet

Additional resources including templates and links inside the spreadsheet.

Have a question, or would like to contact the author?

The My Future Business Show website: https://myfuturebusiness.com

The My Future Business Show email: support@myfuturebusiness.com

Get in front of your best customers on The My Future Business Show. Book your interview below.

https://links.myfuturebusiness.com/interview

Did This Book Help You Launch Your Podcast Marketing System? If yes, please leave your honest review of the book. Appreciate your feedback!

https://links.myfuturebusiness.com/review

How Can I Help You?

Confident you can get podcast marketing results,

but you just don't want to do it on your own?

Then click the link below and let me share how I can help you introduce this proven podcast marketing system into your business without any stress or overwhelm.

https://links.myfuturebusiness.com/podcasting

Made in the USA
Monee, IL
04 November 2026

67380050R00118